TEL F          LIBRARY

# STILL
## THE
## BOSS

## A CANDID LOOK AT BRIAN MULRONEY

0 57812 47211 2

# STILL THE BOSS

# A CANDID LOOK AT BRIAN MULRONEY

## MICHEL GRATTON

Prentice-Hall Canada Inc., Scarborough, Ontario

**Canadian Cataloguing in Publication Data**

Gratton, Michel.
Still the boss

ISBN 0-13-847211-4

1. Mulroney, Brian, 1939-   . 2. Canada - Politics and government -
1984-   .* 3. Prime ministers - Canada - Biography. I. Title.

FC631.M8G73 1990    971.064'7'092    C90-094376-9
F1034.3.M8G73 1990

Prentice-Hall Inc., *Englewood Cliffs, New Jersey*
Prentice-Hall International Inc., *London*
Prentice-Hall of Australia, Pty., *Sydney*
Prentice-Hall of India Pvt. Ltd., *New Delhi*
Prentice-Hall of Japan, Inc., *Tokyo*
Prentice-Hall of Southeast Asia (Pte.) Ltd., *Singapore*
Editora Prentice-Hall do Brasil Ltda., *Rio de Janeiro*
Prentice-Hall Hispanoamericana, S.A., *Mexico*

Editor: William Booth
Design: Monica Kompter
Manufacturing Buyer: Lisa Kreuch
Cover Illustration: Andy Donato
Author Photo: Fred Chartrand

ISBN: 0-13-847211-4

Printed and bound in the U.S.A. by R.R. Donnelley & Sons Company

1 2 3 4 5 RRD 94 93 92 91 90

One more
time with feeling, for
Valerie, Marie-France and
Brigitte;
and for Christine, who
made me believe
in love again.

# Acknowledgements

Special thanks to the people who thought somehow I could do it again: my agent Helen Heller, and all the people at Prentice-Hall, especially Bill Booth, a delightful editor, and Tanya Long, who took the gamble; my love to my friends at the *Sun*, who have been so good and understanding (John Paton, you're not really that fat); my eternal friendship to the Press Gallery's best clerk, John Waterfield, who never, ever, let me down; my apologies to Christine and the girls for being so egotistic (I know I will pay for this); my total gratitude and utter puzzlement at all you people out there who think this is worth reading. Hang on. The adventure is only beginning.

P.S. Mr Creighton, how about another round? On me this time.

## Introduction

"And like a sinner before the gates of heaven, I'll come crawling on back to you."

That unforgettable quote from Meatloaf's famous *Bat Out Of Hell* album kept coming back to me like a prophecy.

I was crawling back, all right, like one who had committed a terrible sin. I was clawing up a cliff to the world where I thought I really belonged: the media. I wasn't even sure they still wanted me, even with an apology.

A political columnist, I had committed the crime of "no-return," by crossing the fence into politics at the highest and most partisan level possible, the prime minister's office. Now, with very little to look forward to, I had thrown that all away.

And I had left, truly, like a bat out of hell. In a fiery flash, as if chased, or even possessed, by demons, I dropped a prestigious job with what I believed to be a fat salary and perks, to go back to...nothing.

Things didn't improve right off the bat, as the reader will find out in the following pages.

After all, I had left behind the man whom many thought could have given me everything, Brian Mulroney. And I then proceeded to cut all bridges between us, by writing a book about it.

*Why?* they asked. *Why do this when you knew of Mulroney's obsession with loyalty, and of his darker, vindictive side?* I looked for a while like a man with a death wish—or a terrible mean streak.

When the book, *"So, What Are The Boys Saying?"* was released—against all odds, I may say—most people favourable to Mulroney were surprised that it didn't taste at all like sour grapes. But they still asked the fundamental question: *Why even do it?*

Well, if they couldn't figure that out with the first book, they're really going to flip over this one.

The first time around, I told those who asked me that question what was obvious to me: I wrote the book because I had a story to tell. The fact that it happened to involve actively the prime minister of the country made it interesting for a lot of Canadians.

But that's all it is. A story. A true one, a human one, sometimes funny, sometimes sad.

That's the way real life is, in the prime minister's office or elsewhere. When the chips are down, Meech Lake, free trade, the GST or any other brilliant scam our politicians can dream up, will not change the fact that, at some point in the day, we all have to go to the toilet.

I didn't set out to destroy any myths but, in the process of explaining how people in high office are no different than the less powerful, I may have done that.

I don't really care. If there are people in a democracy who should never be shielded from public scrutiny, it is precisely those we entrust with power. We give them the greatest gift a human being can give another: our trust.

In return, though, the price they have to pay for earning that trust—and keeping it—is sometimes beyond the call of duty. Politics, in the modern television era, is a dangerous line of work.

Mulroney, for all his setbacks, plays it better than most. He is a consummate politician.

His training may be that of a lawyer, but his heart and mind have always been turned toward learning everything he could about the political game.

This book, for me, was a lot more fun to write than the first.

I could see more clearly.

It took a while, after my passage in the PMO, to recover my true sense of balance, and to be reincarnated into the person I was before my three-year stint in politics.

I don't pass judgement on those who make a life out of it, but the political world was not for me. Being a spokesman for somebody else, keeping my thoughts to myself, guarding my every word was not a life. Not the way I see it, anyway.

Yet, just as Mulroney is fascinated by journalists, I am irresistibly attracted to politicians. They intrigue me.

I tried to stay away, after March, 1987. I told myself that there were other stories, better fun to have, more important battles to fight. Yet, somehow, I could always feel the attraction of the magnet. So I came back.

And, in time, I got to see Brian Mulroney in a more serene and detached way. I saw the people from what we call his "entourage," which I used to be a part of. And I felt for them, deeply. I felt for them every time they were asked to do things that defied logic, to make The Boss look good.

I understood.

I understood when they strained the truth to its limits to protect him, or ran around like a bunch of hyper, little elves, whenever things went wrong and they were trying to salvage the situation. I understood the immense sadness, the empty feeling that comes with every setback.

I also knew when they were trying to fool me.

I was amused by those attempts, just as I was amused by the way some of my colleagues in the media perceived things on "the other side."

That made me discover, over time, that, for the heavy

price I had paid during three years in the political arena, I had acquired something invaluable that few people had: a first-hand look, and knowledge. I knew, without a doubt, what it was like.

When that hit me, I realized also that being free from the shackles of power made me see things very differently. That, of course, included Brian Mulroney himself, whom I was being asked to scrutinize on a daily basis, without worrying about having to throw my body over a grenade to protect him.

I came to understand better a lot of the things that had caused us so much trouble when I was "inside."

And so came the sequel, a second look from the inside and the outside at the man I still call The Boss.

# Chapter 1

"**G**o to West Palm Beach!" he said, happily. "Go see the Expos. Enjoy yourself. Yeah, go to West Palm Beach!"

Funny way for a prime minister to tell you, "You're fired." Only Brian Mulroney could get away with it.

As I, almost mechanically, strolled down from his Parliamentary office, across the Hill's lawn, still covered by the spring's melting snow, I kept repeating to myself those last words of wisdom. A smile might even have come across my face, thinking about Mulroney's unique way of doing things, and about the Florida sun and the Montreal Expos' spring training camp in West Palm.

I had talked about it before with the prime minister, knowing he still prided himself on being an avid baseball fan. But, like his days of drinking and carousing, his passion for sports had ended many years before. It was just one of his ways of being one of the boys again, and pretending that he enjoyed the lighter sides of life, too.

But I always knew he was faking it, that he was too

obsessed with politics and the job of running the country to worry about George Brett's batting average. His telling me to go south, young man, was just his way of saying, "Get the fun out of your system, like I did, before you try doing another serious job..."

I reached my own Press Secretary's office, across Wellington Street in the Langevin Block, where a downcast staff, who had read the writing on the wall a few hours before, were waiting to clean out the office. All I remember is one of the secretaries coming in to tell me a supervisor in the supplies department was wondering if I still had a small portable radio at home that belonged to the government—something worth about a hundred dollars, which I had trekked with from coast to coast for at least a year.

That brought me back to the cold reality of the bureaucracy I had never identified with. She must have known by the look on my face that this was a very bad moment to pursue such an important matter.

She almost ran out of my office, saying simply, "All right, never mind..."

But the request had the benefit of waking me out of my stunned reverie. It was very nice to be free to take holidays in West Palm Beach or elsewhere, but there was one minor matter to take care of: money.

I was out of a job. My only skill was writing, more precisely, journalism. But I had committed the ultimate sin by working, not only on "the other side," but with a politician the media had quickly grown to distrust. And, since I had a well-earned reputation for having an intense repulsion to striped, three-piece suits and short haircuts, I wasn't exactly a prime candidate for the consulting boardrooms of the nation's capital.

Brian Mulroney had once told me, in one of his fatherly talks on board the government's Challenger jet, that when you suffer a political setback, the best thing to do is to get out of Ottawa, go live and work elsewhere. He gave himself as the most successful example of that, since he refused offers to stay in the capital after his first, failed bid for the Tory leadership, in 1976. He also retold the comeback story of Robert Bourassa, who had exiled himself to Europe after Rene Levesque's victory, also in 1976, only to roar back almost a decade later.

Fine and dandy. But I didn't have the connections to make me president of Iron Ore, and besides, my three daughters, still only nine, seven and six years old, were in Ottawa with their mother. Moving was out of the question. So I needed time. And money. Again, Mulroney had said he "would give me the most possible;" that I would be well taken care of. So it was with a certain quiet confidence that I climbed the stairs to the office of the prime minister's chief-of-staff and longtime friend, Bernard Roy, to confirm the details of my death.

Bernard looked like he belonged in a funeral himself. Because, you see, I wasn't the only one. His own assistant, Ian Anderson, and the PM's loyal senior adviser and St. Francis Xavier University friend, Fred Doucet, were to get the bad news. Roy was new at this sort of thing, and his sensitive nature, well-camouflaged by a no-nonsense exterior, couldn't take the hardship coldly—as Mulroney could. He also felt that the firings or resignations within the PMO staff were partly his own fault, since it was his team that the general manager was trading away. And down the road, there would be more to come.

As for me, Bernard had always treated me as a friend more than an employee, and I felt the same way. His secretary, Nicole Guenette, would always let me into his office without an appointment because, she said, "You're the only one who makes him laugh. When you leave, he's in a good mood."

The first moments of our last official meeting were predictably emotional for both of us.

I don't remember what it was I said, but I will never forget his reply. "Don't say any more. I don't want to cry." That was the last thing I wanted, too.

So, about the money.

"I've consulted with the Privy Council Office," Bernard said, taking on his official chief-of-staff tone again, "and, since you offered your resignation, the most we can give you as severance pay is two months."

I must have jumped off my chair when I said, disbe-lievingly, "Two months! You must be kidding! My resig-nation! You're the one who said we should all give the prime minister that option, to make it easy for him. At least I did it!" (As a matter of fact, I still believe I was the only one, at that time, to offer his resignation in writ-ing to Mulroney—Doucet did it by phone.) Getting angri-er by the second, I added, "If I don't get six months' salary, I promise you there will be problems."

Bernard was obviously stunned by my reaction, as he tried to calm me down, saying, "It's okay, it's okay...you'll get what you want, I'll find a way..."

As I went back down to my office, there was Marc Lortie, my eventual successor, waiting for me. Marc was an experienced bureaucrat and diplomat—a resource I had had to pipe in often, during the previous three years, because of my own ignorance of the public-service uni-verse.

"Six months is the least you should get...plus your holidays," said Lortie, sympathetically.

He promised to fight for me and, knowing Marc, I believed he would do exactly that.

That same night, Brian Mulroney phoned Lortie to ask him to become his new press secretary—the fourth in his less than four years as Tory leader. Mulroney told him he was acting on my personal recommendation.

That hurt, because it was only partly true. I had rec-ommended Lortie for the job, but to Bernard Roy. Now the PM claimed that he had discussed it with me, which he never had. I thought to myself, *That's Mulroney all right...rearranging situations to make them happen the right way, and then convincing other people of their authenticity.* I had never really imagined I would be a victim of it, though.

Marc also told me the prime minister said he had had enough of an "event-oriented" communications approach, what Communications Director Bill Fox used to call "blue smoke and mirrors." Mulroney now wanted to be seen as a man of substance. He obviously thought somebody like me couldn't handle substantial matters. *What a guy*, I thought. *Not only does he put me out on the street without knowing how much severance pay I'm getting, but he craps all over me on the night of the burial.* Where was this class he was supposed to have? The class he boasted about when he closed down the northern Quebec mining town of Shefferville, as head of Iron Ore. I guess I was a little angry. And the precariousness of my situation was starting to dawn on me.

The following night, I went to my favourite watering hole, the National Press Club, where the whole PMO adventure had started, three years earlier. I was doing some commiserating with a couple of journalists, among others Joe O'Donnell, then with *The Toronto Star*, Bob Fife, then with CP, and Jan Lounder, from the *Sun*, when all of a sudden, a bottle of beer came flying between Jan and me, about one inch from my head, and crashed into the glass and bottles on the other side of the bar. I turned, to look at a very drunk Gerry McNeil, a veteran CP reporter, who was one of the mildest, nicest people around until that proverbial one too many. He had his fists up and was taunting me. He was in no shape to fight, but I was in no mood to take abuse.

As it turned out, nothing happened, but the next day in *The Toronto Sun*, columnist Derik Hodgson wrote about "the violence" that had happened at the Club the night before, insinuating that I had provoked it. I hadn't said a word to McNeil who, by the way, apologized profusely the next day, and has been a model of restraint ever since that regrettable night. But I couldn't believe how, once again, the facts could be distorted in such a way, by the same reporter who, four months earlier, had practically fabricated a story making me into a sex harasser.

I asked myself, *Is this ever going to end?*

That day, the PMO had put out a terse press release, saying I was "returning to the private sector." My friends eagerly joked about it, as I admitted that "private sector" might just mean "unemployment."

In the days that followed, the phone kept ringing.

But one of the most memorable calls came from Luc Lavoie, who, paradoxically, less than two years down the road, was going to be a crucial member of Mulroney's reelection team. Lavoie was then chief-of-staff to Energy Minister Marcel Masse. He was mad too.

He offered the condolences of his maverick minister, adding, "You know, he really likes you. What is really disgusting in your firing is that they picked the only one who couldn't harm them, the most expendable, to make an example. You are neither from the Big Blue Machine, nor a Quebec Tory, nor one of Mulroney's old buddies. It stinks."

It struck me that he might have been right. As calculating as Mulroney was, he probably had weighed all those things.

But the most important conversation, in retrospect, had to be the one I had with television superstar Mike Duffy.

"You have to write a book. You'll make some dough, and it will bring you back in the journalism business," he said.

"Mulroney won't like it," I said.

"It doesn't have to be nasty, and it can't be sour grapes," Mike said.

"You don't know him," I replied, prophetically.

Duffy then set out to find me a publisher, and also put his friend, Peter Mansbridge, Canada's foremost anchorman, on the job. I knew Peter, but I couldn't have claimed, at the time, that he was a friend of mine. He had no good reason to help and besides, he didn't need anybody's favours.

So I was rather surprised when, out of the blue, I got a call from Toronto, and the familiar night-time voice came on the line. Mansbridge had found me an agent. For the next six months, Nancy Colbert, known then as the best literary agent in Toronto, would act as my new-found mother.

But I still wasn't convinced I should write the book. Then Charles Lynch phoned me, to ask how I was doing. I had always had tremendous respect for the dean of

Canada's political columnists, and I told him about the book.

"Listen," he said, "you only get so many kicks at the can."

I started to work on an outline.

I was rusty. It just wasn't coming out. I started believing I had lost it. Three years away from the typewriter had been too much. Then it happened, in the middle of the night. I woke up, and it was all clear. I had dreamt of *"So, What Are the Boys Saying?"* I sat down in front of my old Underwood at three in the morning.

Somehow I felt like I had crossed the Rubicon. There was no turning back, and soon I would have Brian Mulroney as a formidable enemy.

So, I figured I'd better settle my severance pay problems before making another move. Bernard Roy informed me I would get my six months; two months paid for by the government, two months by the Conservative party, and nine weeks holidays owed to me. I smiled. He had said six months, but he was really talking four. I thanked him anyway, knowing already that chances were he'd regret his "generosity" a few weeks down the road.

Then I went to West Palm Beach.

But that wasn't before managing to lose the Tory party severance cheque for some $12,000. It was the first time I'd ever lost a cheque in my life, and it had to be that one. The Tory party, however, was more than accommodating, as it cancelled the first and issued a new one, in a matter of hours. I felt like a jackass. And I could just hear them in the smoke-filled rooms, saying, "Boy weren't we right to get rid of that clumsy idiot?"

But I was also amazed at how easy it was to get the money. I had seen a lot of strange transactions go through the PC Canada Fund over my three years in the PMO, but I was still impressed at the easy access the Tory powerbrokers had to cash.

The first cheque mysteriously resurfaced months later, and Conservative Party director Jean-Carol

Pelletier, who is still a friend, told me with a smile, "When you lose a cheque, it's not a small one."

West Palm Beach was all right. Lots of old ladies with blue hair on the beach, two of whom mistook me for comic actor Robin Williams, coming up to me and saying, "Should I know you?"

The Expos were playing well, but the beer and hot dogs were the best. The hotel was a dump, and I made a bet with my friend Gilles Pilon, on how many days our room service trays would be left out in the hallway, before they were picked up. One was left there for two days...but we found it on the floor below, as we were going down the stairs. They had just moved it, so we'd stop complaining.

But things were looking up. Pilon was now an editor at my old paper, Ottawa's daily *Le Droit*, and they had already approached me to start writing a column again. I had money in the bank and an outline being passed around to publishers. More importantly, I had a bottle of rum and a beautiful view of the ocean.

Then came the phone call. I was a little taken aback. Who on earth could be phoning us here? Must be room service.

A familiar, nasal, female voice came on the line. "Monsieur Gratton, the Prime Minister of Canada would like to speak to you."

My friend Pilon couldn't help but see the stupefaction on my face.

"Who is it?" he asked.

"The prime minister," I stuttered.

"Salut, mon Michel," said the deep voice.

"Mister prime minister," I answered dutifully, as I always had, and still do.

"Where are you now?"

"Where you told me to go...West Palm Beach."

"How are the Expos doing?"

"Uh...I think they're doing much better than people say they are. They beat the Dodgers today."

"Good...I remember, years ago, when I used to go. We'd go to the ballpark and then, nine beers later..." He then bellowed out his trademark laugh, and added, "I just wanted to know how you were."

After I hung up, Pilon asked me, "What on earth did he want?"

"He just wanted to know how the Expos and I were doing."

"You mean the Prime Minister of Canada phoned you for that! That's incredible. That's bizarre."

"That's Mulroney," I said.

There was a pause. Then Gilles said, "Does he know you're writing a book?"

I just stared out at the ocean and poured myself another rum.

# Chapter 2

I was dozing on the couch, when the phone rang.

After three years in the PMO, I believed I had developed a sixth sense about the sound of the ring. Or maybe it was simply that it often seemed to happen when you expected it the least. But somehow, I felt it was HIM.

I had been back from West Palm Beach for a few weeks, and my departure from the PMO was already more than a month behind me. I was working on the book. It wasn't easy. Politics had made my writing rusty, and I couldn't bear to read myself. As a result, I kept starting over.

We were on the edge of signing a publishing contract for a fall release, but my agent kept running into the incredulity of publishers, who thought it couldn't be done. Most wanted to go in the spring. I steadfastly refused, because I firmly believed the book wouldn't have any relevance a year later. Besides, it was only a matter of time before Mulroney found out, if he didn't know already. The less time he had to react, the better. Nancy Colbert was urging me to write anyway, confident somebody would buy the idea, but it was hard for me to do it without a contract in hand.

The phone must have rung five or six times. It wasn't ringing as often in those days, as only the real friends were checking up on the life of a failed press secretary.

When I finally picked it up, I almost expected the response at the other end. "Monsieur Gratton, the prime minister would like to speak to you."

God, what does he want this time? I thought. This was only our third conversation since my departure. The second had come at the annual Press Gallery Dinner, and had been as innocuous as the West Palm Beach one. Little did I suspect then, that this was going to be the last time we would talk in a long while.

"Michel," he said, after the usual salutations, "I've been talking with Fred (Doucet), and I think you should go and see him. He may have something for you. You've got to form yourself a little company, that's what you have to do."

Fred Doucet, by then, had been appointed Canadian Ambassador to the Summits, an impressive title created by Mulroney for the fallen buddy he had decided to kick out of his PMO shortly after me. It meant that he was the PM's top representative for the organization of the three upcoming summits Canada was scheduled to host within a year: the Francophone Summit in Quebec City in September, the Commonwealth Summit in Vancouver in October, and the Economic Summit in Toronto the following spring. It was an important job, because the prime minister was counting a lot on the massive media exposure from those international events to boost his re-election fortunes. Although, in a conversation weeks before my departure, Mulroney had confided in me that he was starting to doubt the electoral value of hosting such monstrous events. Remember, at that time, he was only at a little more than twenty percent in the popularity polls.

Nevertheless, I must say it came as something of a shock that he would ask me to be part of his team one more time. But I was pretty sure I didn't want it.

"Mister prime minister," I answered, "I appreciate your concern, but I'm not sure I'd like to return to public life, for the moment. I think I've had more than enough of it."

Undaunted, he went on. "Come on, Michel. They can't hold it against us, because we seek some professional help. Give Fred a call—and form a company."

I hung up, still mesmerized by how the man's mind worked. "They" can't hold it against us, he had said. Who were "they?" He could only have meant the media, the enemy. He obviously thought, in his egocentric way, that I didn't want him to be harmed by my going to work with Fred, when all the time, I was really concerned with my own sanity. I shook my head in disbelief, and muttered to myself that he would never understand.

I didn't phone Fred. He phoned me, a few days later.

"Michel, has The Boss phoned you?" He sounded almost embarrassed.

"Yeah...he said he wanted me to go see you. Said something about a company."

"Yeah, I know...uh, why don't you come by tomorrow or some other time..." I did. Partly because I was curious, partly because his office was just down the street from where I lived in Vanier, on the bank of the Rideau River.

It was nice to see Fred, a short, grey-haired man with a voice like Barney Rubble, and a demeanour to match. He had been much maligned by the media during his stay in the PMO, but I had often thought that his only sin was to be fiercely loyal to Mulroney. He wouldn't admit the man's most obvious failings.

He greeted me with a large smile, as we sat down in his penthouse office for a coffee. He said he was bored, and that he missed the action in the PMO. I realized that there, in front of me, sat a very sad man. Also a very bitter one. He started to talk about his last days in the PMO, and how Bernard Roy hadn't even bothered to come and see him in his office just down the hall.

"He didn't say a word to me! Not a word!" He was hurting.

It felt awful to see someone I had been through the

wars with cast aside like a dirty rag. All of a sudden, I felt that my pain was very small, compared to his. At least, I didn't feel betrayed by my friends. For me, it had just been an adventure. For Fred, getting to the prime minister's office was the accomplishment of his life.

He suddenly lightened up, saying, "But Brian phoned me!" That was all he seemed to need, to go on; a little pat on the back from his friend, the prime minister.

Speaking of the prime minister, I thought, how about the matter at hand?

I took the opening he was giving me, and said, "Fred, I spoke with The Boss. Now just tell me, what is it you think I could do here?"

He looked at me as if I'd hit the nail right on the head, and gave the frankest answer he could. "I don't know."

I felt a rage rush to my face, as I thought that that was precisely the kind of thing Mulroney thought he could get away with. Just dump all your losers in the same place, so they'll know Brian will take care of them for the rest of their lives. The network of the Godfather.

I explained to Fred that I didn't see how I could be useful, when I knew darn well the upcoming Francophone Summit already had an excess of press secretaries from all levels of government. Fred nodded, and we parted friends.

One of the last things I said to him (and I really meant it as a warning) was, "I have to play to my strengths. And that's writing."

He concluded the meeting by saying, "Well, if you can think of something you could do...," but he didn't believe it. He added, "You will always be my friend."

That night, I had a conversation with a girlfriend I was in the process of breaking up with—hey, if you're gonna quit, might as well go all the way. I told her how Mulroney just wanted to keep people under his influence, how he wanted to make sure they'd depend on him for the rest of their lives. I said I'd rather starve than depend on somebody else.

"What's wrong with that?" she said. It may have had

something to do with the fact that she was still working in the PMO.

I sighed. Now I knew I was alone.

Nancy Colbert signed me up with a publisher shortly after that, thanks to a young Toronto editor by the name of Denise Schon who, for no good reason, thought I could do it. All she had seen was the outline. I'm not sure we were all fully conscious, at the time, of the forces we were unleashing. She thought she'd sell books; I knew I would have to go through rough waters before that would happen.

It didn't take long for the boat to start rocking.

Everything was triggered by a short, gossipy item in *Maclean's* magazine.

I was scheduled to be a featured speaker at a roast for my friend Bill Fox, at the National Arts Centre, a few days later. The official pretext for the event was Foxie's fortieth birthday but, for most people, it was a show of support for the man who had just suddenly resigned from the PMO, as a result of pressure from Mulroney's new chief-of-staff, the ruthless Derek Burney. The prime minister had let it happen, after promising Fox, two months earlier, that he was going to be the new gate-keeper, handling every communication between the PM, the government, and the outside world.

Fox had been first Press Secretary (I was his deputy), then Director of Communications. But in that tumul-tuous spring of 1987, the prime minister had offered him the new job, mainly because he wanted to bring in well-known media and TV figure Bruce Phillips from the Washington embassy, where he acted as press attache to Ambassador Allan Gotlieb, as communication director.

Why Phillips? Mulroney had been convinced, by members of the Big Blue Machine, that the dignified image of the man who had been CTV Ottawa bureau chief and commentator for years would be more prof-itable to him than Fox's bull-in-the-china-shop number. Little did he know that Fox and Phillips were both very much of the same no-nonsense mould. And it was ironic—but not surprising to me—that Bruce Phillips would himself be treated like a pariah before the next election came along, and then sidelined to another job. It is very much Brian Mulroney's way of governing that, when the part doesn't work, you simply get a new one.

In any case, Bill Fox was to be kicked upstairs, with an office right on the doorstep of the prime minister's. (He booted a guy named Geoff Norquay out of that one.)

I had supper at his place shortly after my resignation. Bonnie Brownlee, Mila Mulroney's executive assistant and now Fox's wife, was also present, as was my former secretary, Ann Charron. It was then that Bill explained to me what The Boss was offering him.

"What are you going to do?" I asked.

"I dunno," he said. "Somehow the job doesn't seem as great to me as he makes it sound."

Later, he asked what I thought he should do.

I looked at a man I have always had immense respect for, straight in the eyes, and said, "Get the hell out of there, before it's too late."

Bonnie Brownlee confided in me, a long time after the encounter, that she had never forgotten those words.

It wasn't long after that, that things turned sour for the proud Fox. Derek Burney took over, and he knew that the only way to get control of the PMO operation was to get his own people in place. There were a few untouchables, but none as powerful and influential as Fox. He was dangerous to the career bureaucrat, who knew darned well that, if it wasn't the prime minister calling Fox at home every night, it would be Mila phoning Bonnie.

So, as the story was told to me, once he felt he had sufficient power to do so, he called Fox into his Langevin Block office. He basically asked him to explain what his responsibilities were. Dutifully, Fox explained how he was expected to screen the communications to and from the PM.

Burney answered simply, "No. I do that."

Fox felt there was nothing left for him to do but leave. Burney had read him right. He knew Fox was too proud to go begging for a job. Burney also knew he was exhausted after three years on Mulroney's roller-coaster, and demoralized by the turn of events.

Fox quit, and he didn't even ask for a severance agreement. I told him he was out of his mind. He thought maybe he was. He and I also knew—although I never brought it up with him—that, as long as Bonnie was working for Mila, Brian Mulroney knew he had him on a string.

Fox is now an extremely successful consultant in Ottawa. But, trust me, it has very little to do with what Mulroney did for him. Paradoxically, if anybody helped him out, it was guys from the Big Blue Machine, like Harry Near, who knew his real value. But most of it he did himself, with that dogged Irish determination that turns human beings into driven cannonballs.

But on that night in June, at the Arts Centre, Fox and his intimates were keeping all of this drama to themselves, as a few hundred well-wishers showed up to show their friendship—okay, there may have been a few hypocrites in the bunch. Ian L. MacDonald, a former columnist for *The Montreal Gazette*, author of Mulroney's first biography, and then his speechwriter, was the master of ceremonies.

And guess who was the star speaker and guest? Right, The Boss.

Mulroney had just returned from the Venice Economic Summit, and I was told in advance that he would be there.

"Is he going to stay for the speeches?" I asked eagerly.

In a strange way, I wanted him to hear mine. I was told they didn't know about him, but that Mila was expected to tough the run.

When he came into the hall, to sit at the table of honour next to the man he had just allowed to be canned by an External Affairs bureaucrat, the prime minister never looked my way. I was only two tables away. But his wife did. And her expression meant, *What have you been doing, bad boy?*

It was the first hint I got that they would not be pleased, or even amused, by the possibility of me becoming an author at their expense.

Still, I went through with my prepared speech, after Ian MacDonald introduced me as the Great Gratsky. The prime minister had left by then, but his wife was still there.

I started my address by saying I was happy to take time away from writing my book. The crowd laughed, but not the head table.

I also said to Fox, in the good roasting tradition, "Fox, remember when you told me, during the election campaign that, if we blew a ten-point lead in the polls, our heads would be the first impaled on the spiked fence of Parliament Hill by the Big Blue Machine? Well, we won. What have you got to say for yourself now, smartass?"

Fox knew it was a joke, but there were people in the room, like Bernard Roy, who started to squirm on their chairs.

As I left the hall that night, I bumped into Bonnie Brownlee, who had been sitting next to Mila, and asked rather inoffensively, "Was my speech okay?"

"Yeah, it was all right," she said, looking away.

That was not her normal behaviour.

I knew something was up. Another roast. And I was the meal.

**Chapter** 3

First came the letter.

It wasn't long, but it said it all. I took it as a warning, almost a threat.

The crucial paragraph read, "My wife and I have always appreciated your unflinching loyalty." It was signed by Brian Mulroney.

I was flabbergasted. This was totally out of character for the prime minister, who was well-known for using the telephone for most of his important conversations. It was both safer and quicker than putting something down on paper and sending it through the mail.

It was also pretty stupid and careless, for a man who prided himself on "strategizing" his every move. In fact, had I been as disloyal as the prime minister would later make me out to be, semi-privately, after the release of "So, What Are The Boys Saying?" I would have used that letter to boost sales of the book. It was the most positive proof, in black and white, that Mulroney himself had tried to stop me from writing it, as soon as he had definitely found out about it a few days earlier, at Fox's party. But for him to take such a chance meant two things: he was damned angry, and dead serious about using every means at his disposal to stop me.

I gulped at the prospect of having to take on, not only the prime minister of the country, but one of the most vengeful and unforgiving persons I'd ever known.

I was shaken. Mulroney could only have done this in a blind rage, because he obviously wasn't thinking straight.

Nevertheless, I was relieved he hadn't tried to get me by phone. I'm not sure I would have been able to stand up to him.

Bernard Roy took care of that. He called to invite me out to dinner. I knew I was in for a fun night.

We drove to a Hull restaurant called Le Picodon in his Chrysler. It was only the second time we'd had dinner together, just the two of us. We'd done it once before in the early days of the mandate. It had been a terrific night at L'Oree du bois, where a bond seemed to have formed between Bernard and I. He thought he had found a friend in a city he still finds very alien and cold. But on this night, I'm afraid neither of us was too sure where that friendship stood any more. Not too many words were exchanged in the car.

After sitting down in front of a bottle of Beaujolais, Bernard didn't waste any time in getting it off his chest. That was his way; he liked to get to the point. That was fine with me, since I'm the same and I knew the air was getting thicker by the minute between us.

"I listened to your speech the other night at Fox's party," he started out by saying. "It was a good speech, by the way. One could tell you had prepared it. But I also told my wife after, 'Michel sounds bitter'."

I kept quiet. I wanted to hear the whole spiel first. He went on to talk about the book, of course, and informed me that he had found out who my publisher was.

"Jesus, you guys work fast!" I said.

"No. I just happened to bump into a party member from Toronto, who had heard about it."

*Sure*, I thought. *You didn't send out your spies on a mission. Oh no, Mulroney wouldn't do that.* But I held back from saying anything. It would only have produced a sterile argument.

"Needless to say, the prime minister and I are very disappointed and worried that you have decided to do this."

"What are you afraid of?"

"All kinds of things you could reveal, inside information you were privy to and that, by the way, you were entrusted with."

"Like what?"

"Say you write that he thinks the premier of Alberta, Don Getty, is a son of a bitch. What will that do for federal-provincial relations?"

"You're worried I'll mess up federal-provincial relations?" I said, incredulously.

"I'm just giving that as an example of the damage it could cause."

"Can I say he doesn't like Howard Pawley?" I asked jokingly, speaking of the Manitoba NDP premier Mulroney was feuding with at the time.

Bernard didn't laugh. He was getting impatient, probably because he felt he was getting nowhere. Of course, the subject was a rather sensitive one at the time, since Mulroney was on the verge of pulling off the Meech Lake Accord. But that would happen long before the publication of my book.

Bernard then went on to say that, after everything the prime minister had done for me, after what he had shared with me, after the opportunity he had given me, he didn't deserve such a betrayal.

"If what you're telling me is that I owe something to Brian Mulroney, my own view of it is that we're pretty even," I said.

"All right," replied Bernard, defiantly, "let's make a box-score of what you two have done for each other. Okay, you joined him before the election, when he was fifteen points down in the polls. That's one point in your favour."

"Thanks."

"But then, when you got in trouble, in the fall of '86, he could have fired you then. He didn't. He even ordered the party to pay for your lawyer's bill."

"What else was he supposed to do? Am I any worse than Sinc Stevens? Besides, it didn't amount to anything, and it wasn't my suggestion, it was your own suggestion that you get me a lawyer to sue the newspaper. And I hadn't done anything wrong!"

"All right. But what about your severance pay? You got six months."

"Yeah. Nine weeks holidays owed to me, included in that."

"That's true," he said, softly. He stopped talking.

I picked it up. I was starting to feel bad about the whole thing. This man was my friend, and he just couldn't get himself to move in for the kill. He couldn't carry out the contract.

So I said, apologetically, "Look, Bernard, even if I wanted to stop writing the book, I couldn't. It's too late. I've already cashed in the advance from the publisher."

"Well, if you haven't spent it, you can return it."

"With the debts I've got!"

The conversation had come to a dead end.

Finally I said to him, "What if the book is a positive one?"

He looked at me, wide-eyed, and burst out laughing, a good hearty laugh, his first of the evening.

"Knowing you," he said, still chuckling, "you're gonna say it the way it was."

I joined in the laughter. Thoughts about those weird things Mulroney would do and say were going through our minds.

We didn't discuss the book after that. Rather, he started lecturing me on the way I treated women. He was referring to the fact that, the week before, I had been spotted walking in front of the PMO offices—where my former girlfriend still worked—with "a gorgeous blonde."

"You can never humiliate women," he said, in a fatherly way.

I didn't have the heart to tell him that, in that relationship, I was the one being humbled. She had left me.

He dropped me off at a Hull bar. Before getting out of the car, I said to him, half-jokingly, "To our next quarrel."

"There was no quarrel," he replied.

I never knew what he thought of that night or whether, as far as he was concerned, he had accomplished his mission. But I have to admit I was rattled. If he couldn't stop me from writing, maybe he had done the second best thing: kept me from being too hard on the prime minister, or revealing things that would be too embarrassing.

In the next few days, Bill Fox would try to reach me repeatedly. For the first time ever, I would not return his phone calls. I knew what they were about, and I was terrified that another confrontation like the one I'd had with Bernard would finish me off. I'd never write the book.

The only time Fox had tried to discuss it was at lunch in the Byward Market, where I'd confided in him that I had written that he hired me on a drunk.

"Maybe that's not the way you should write it..." he started to say.

I apologized to him for not being in the mood to discuss it at that moment, since I had just had another big fight with my girlfriend.

Classy as he always was, he conceded, "I guess this is not the time." We ended up reading the menu and drinking half a twelve pack each, before wrapping up our "lunch." (Fox, to his credit, has now been on the wagon for more than two years.)

But if he was calling me now, two weeks later, it was assuredly because he was getting some kind of pressure from The Boss himself. And Bonnie was probably getting it from Mila. So the last thing I wanted was to be faced with a man that I knew to be more persuasive than Bernard.

It also dawned on me at that moment that Mulroney was doing all of this pretty cleverly: he was using two of the people I loved the most in his entourage to try to get to me.

In the days that followed, other pressure came from just about everywhere. I could hardly find a friend who didn't disagree with my writing the book—let alone enemies. I was seriously starting to doubt. How could I be right, and the rest of the world wrong? It reminded me of what my mother used to tell me, when she got fed up with my arrogance and stubborness.

"Michel Gratton, you think everybody's a fool but you!"

I was having more and more trouble writing. I had started out doing a chapter a day. Now I could hardly bang out a page. I started drinking heavily, from morning to night. I wasn't writing a line, and I couldn't face life sober. Until, after a week of idle drinking, mostly alone in my apartment, I ended up in the hospital with a heavy nosebleed that wouldn't stop. It scared the hell out of me, as I had trouble breathing and I thought I was going to die.

It scared me so much that I quite drinking altogether, and sat down at the typewriter again. I remember my editor phoning and asking how things were going. I said everything was peachy.

"Good. I just wanted to make sure you were not out drinking beer all day or something."

I didn't say anything. I just wanted to get back to work. But my heart still wasn't in it, until something happened to change it all around.

Ironically, that event could have been the last blow, had I been in a different frame of mind. I was having lunch at the Press Club with one of my best friends, Maurice Godin, who had come down from Quebec City, where he was working for Mulroney's Francophone Summit—a job I had made sure he got. When the people we were with left, Maurice said he had something to tell me.

"I'm not sure if I should tell you," he said, "but you're my friend."

I waited, expecting the worst, as he said simply, "Ann phoned me."

"What did she want?" I asked about my former

girlfriend—I still had strong feelings for her—who was back working in the PMO.

"She's afraid for you, because of the book. She's afraid you're gonna get hurt. That people who love you will end up hating you."

I must have turned red with rage. How could she do that? She had been on my side all along. There was only one explanation: the pressure inside must have been unbearable.

I won't go into the phone conversation I had with her after that. I know now that she was genuinely concerned about me, and I regret some of the things I said. But I couldn't believe that, somehow, she had been dragged into it too, and was phoning my best friend in Quebec City to try and knock some sense into me.

They had made a crucial mistake. They got me mad.

That night, I returned home in a mood to kill. In the days that followed, I banged out copy like a man possessed.

I only got one more phone call from a real PMO friend, who I can't identify. That person told me, "Watch yourself. You're driving them to the brink of sanity in here. Make sure you have doubles of everything you do, and keep them in a safe place. Not in your home."

At first, I shrugged it off. Then I started to think; what could they do? An injunction? What if, somehow, they could prove I was in possession of national secrets, or simply government documents? What if they decided to confiscate the manuscript, claiming I was revealing matters of national security or God knows what?

Nah...They wouldn't be that dumb.

I discussed it briefly with a friend, who asked me point-blank, "The point is, do you think they're capable of it?"

I didn't have to think very long to find the answer to that. "Yes, if they're desperate enough...but it would be crazy."

I would learn much later, from two different sources, that the matter of legal intervention to prevent the release of the book had been discussed within the PMO.

How serious was it and who was giving the orders? Obviously, it didn't go very far, and cooler heads prevailed. They understood that such action would only cause the book to become an instant bestseller, maybe internationally, as *Spycatcher* turned out to be, when Margaret Thatcher banned its publication in England.

All I know is that the PMO friend who had warned me, had to have a reason to do so.

I made sure I followed his advice. To this day, I still have some copies of the manuscript that I never retrieved.

I finished the book just a few days past deadline. I was laughing. I was going back to work at *Le Droit* as a columnist-at-large, and Brian Mulroney was behind me.

I should have known better.

**Chapter 4**

God, how I hate to write those "Hi, it's me" columns.

But I accept that they're a necessary evil whenever a new columnist is introduced to the readers. In my case, in August, 1987, it was more a case of the prodigal son returning home after a three-year adventure in politics. *Le Droit*, the paper that had made a parliamentary columnist out of me in the first place—which had led to my meeting Brian Mulroney—had taken me back like the father in the Bible story.

I was slated to write a column at large that did not exclude federal politics. In my first column, I decided to use something my eldest daughter, Valerie, had written about me for the previous Father's Day.

Apart from telling a few white lies, such as that I was an excellent cook, Valerie had written that "I had invented a book."

I thought it was a beautiful expression, and I comented on it by saying that, when he read it, Brian Mulroney himself would probably say that I had "invented" a book. I simply thought it was a funny way of saying that he wouldn't believe a word of it, and tell people that.

Well, what happened next just shows you how touchy the man who runs the country was about the whole subject. He must have choked on his coffee that morning, when he anxiously turned to *Le Droit*'s page three to read, for the first time, what I had to say—if anything—about his right honourable person.

Minutes after he read it, he was on the phone to his press secretary, Marc Lortie, saying, "What's he gonna do? Tell lies about my wife and I?"

It didn't take long for Lortie to get in touch with me and repeat the prime minister's concern—as he was probably told to do.

"For God's sake, Marc, it was a joke!"

He chuckled. He had known it all along, but he also knew that you don't try to reason with Mulroney when he's in a highly excited state—that's putting it mildly.

After I hung up the phone, I thought to myself, *Is this the way it's going to be forever? A fight to the finish between him and me, because I did something he didn't like.* Maybe it was. And it was only starting.

Mulroney's attitude about my upcoming book was affecting the whole PMO. As The Boss goes, so they go. That's the way he wants it. If he's worried, everybody has to worry. If he's happy, everybody's happy.

During those tense summer days, however, as it was described to me by several people on the inside, the place was close to panic at the prospect of my book sending the government into a tailspin, just when it had started its recovery from a plunge to twenty-three percent in the popularity polls. At boardroom meetings, Bernard Roy would talk about "those so-called friends of ours, who have become our enemies."

What didn't help was all the media hype around it, and another upcoming book, Claire Hoy's *Friends in High Places*, which everybody knew was going to be highly critical of the prime minister.

The advance stories on my book left the clear impression that it was going to be a devastatingly true account of life with Brian Mulroney in power. Former colleagues were being quoted anonymously as saying things about me like, "if he says one word about me, I'll sue."

I guess I didn't help much in an interview with the *Star*'s Joe O'Donnell. In response to a question, asking what I would do if former PMO colleagues contested what I had written, I said, "Go ahead, make my day."

During those tense days, Mulroney would often rant and rave about me in front of aides and ministers, calling me a "traitor"—usually screaming, as only he can.

In at least one instance, I was told that he said, "If I can make trouble for him, you can bet I will..."

One of his aides assured me, however, that he wasn't serious about it. "You know he'd never do anything...He was just mouthing off."

Oh yeah? Well, I'm not too sure about that.

A disturbing incident that took place in my early days at *Le Droit* leads me to believe that there was more fire than smoke to Mulroney's menace.

I had been at the paper about a month. The publisher, Gilbert Lacasse, asked me to take part in some official function to show the flag, something that I have always considered to be part of a columnist's job. After the event, in Hull, Lacasse invited me and two editors to go have a few more late drinks at a local bar, Aux Quatre Jeudis.

Before I go into what happened next, it's important for the reader to know that a major change in ownership had happened at *Le Droit* almost simultaneously with my arrival. The paper, along with the two others in the Unimedia chain, Quebec's *Le Soleil* and Chicoutimi's *Le Quotidien*, had been bought by none other than newspaper magnate, writer, and billionaire extraordinaire Conrad Black. Now Black could not be called a Mulroney intimate, although the two men know each other well. But they sort of gravitate in the same circles.

More importantly however, the man Black put in charge of the Unimedia chain, his longtime buddy Peter White, is also a very close friend of Brian Mulroney's. The debonair White was one of the prime minister's closest advisers, in both his 1983 leadership and 1984 election campaigns. He was the first person put in charge of patronage in Mulroney's original PMO. And, although he lasted barely two years in the job—he switched over to Black's empire—he was to be appointed principal secretary to the prime minister, replacing Bernard Roy, in the summer of 1988, just before the re-election bid.

Although I always thought of White as a very pleasant, ever-smiling, intelligent person, I also had no doubt about his ruthlessness. But I honestly never thought I would be on the short end of it.

So much for background.

We had been at the Quatre Jeudis bar for a good while. We were not counting the beers, but recounting more and more good stories. Lips were getting loose, at the risk of sinking a few ships. Lacasse, news editor Gilles Pilon, night editor Claude Tremblay and I were going at it the way newsroom people do, when they get the chance to speak their minds to the publisher—and vice-versa.

The words were blunt, and the conversation was frank. But I never expected in my wildest imagination to hear the confession the publisher was about to make.

"You know," he said, "Unimedia didn't want me to hire you."

"What do you mean?" I said.

"Well, shortly after you started writing, I had a meeting with Pierre Desmarais (head of Unimedia, not related to the Desmarais Power Corporation family). He told me he didn't think it was a wise decision to have you as a columnist."

I didn't know this Desmarais guy from a hole in the ground, and I was pretty sure he knew very little, if anything, about my skills as a columnist. More than that, I don't think he cared. Why single me out?

The answer came from Lacasse. It was with an almost mischievous twinkle in his eyes that he went on. "I asked him why he thought so. After a little prodding, he said that Peter White had told him to make the message."

"What did you say?" I asked, while the two other editors listened in amazement.

"I said I thought you were good for the paper...he never raised it after that."

The next morning, when I awoke with the beer foam clouding my brain, I wondered if I hadn't dreamt it all. When I saw my friend Pilon in the newsroom that night, I asked him if he had heard the same story I had. He confirmed it.

"Goddam Mulroney," I muttered.

Months later, Lacasse would repeat the identical story in front of other witnesses and myself at the National Press Club's sixtieth anniversary night.

Well, I have a long memory too. And, trying to get to the bottom of it, I raised the whole incident in July of '88, with Bernard Roy, days after he finally resigned from the PMO and he felt free to speak to me again.

We had lunch at a restaurant called Victor's on the corner of Elgin and Queen. Bernard was a little under the weather since, the night before, he had been treated to a farewell party in the Senate Speaker's dining room. He is not much of a drinker or party-goer. As he once told me, "I drink, but I watch myself."

I was already into my second aperitif beer when he showed up and ordered a Perrier, saying to the server, "I did a little excess last night."

To which I replied, "I didn't...or maybe I'm more used to it."

"That's exactly what I was going to say," he added, laughing. "But I did have a few gins too many with your buddies, Luc Lavoie and Paul Terrien (two of Mulroney's advisers and former journalists). As a matter of fact, they even dragged me to the Press Club looking for you, around midnight."

He then quickly went into an apology that I didn't think was needed at all. "I'm sorry if I didn't call you or speak to you for the last year...but the circumstances were such, you know..."

"Don't worry about it. You have no excuses to make," I said.

"I must tell you honestly I am still disappointed in the fact that you wrote the book. I don't think you should have done it. That being said, however, I thought it was rather mild...and I thank you for the kind words you had for me."

"I meant it."

That was all very nice, but it was then my turn to get something off my chest. I told him about what had happened at *Le Droit*, Peter White's intervention, which I suspected had been telegraphed from The Boss himself.

Bernard looked down at his Perrier glass for a moment, and all he said was, "You have to understand that those were very difficult days for us, and the prime minister. The hype in the papers led us to believe it would be very negative."

"That's no reason to try and prevent a guy from earning a living."

He never confirmed or denied it. To me, his silence was eloquent enough.

But, to come back to the fall of 1987, all this behind-the-scenes hysteria in the PMO was going on even before the book was made public. About a month before the book launch, I decided to make a cameo appearance at the Francophone Summit in Quebec City. It was to be the first time I would attend a Mulroney event on the journalists' side of the fence, since my March departure from the PMO.

I wasn't looking to make any trouble, except on the social side of things, where I succeeded brilliantly. I was interested in the summit, but I really was looking forward to getting reacquainted with some old friends.

I attended the major closing press conference that Mulroney was giving as chairman of the Summit, along with Francophone leaders, among them the President of France, Francois Mitterrand. It was the first time I had seen him in person since the previous Gallery Dinner. It felt funny to look from a distance at a man I had been so close to all those years.

I deliberately sat in the very last row of the room

filled by several hundred journalists from Canada and around the world. I didn't want to antagonize him.

But guess who suddenly showed up, and sat next to me? Mulroney's executive assistant, Rick Morgan. I was immensely pleased to see him. He had been, in the PMO, one of my favourite people—and still is. For a twenty-four-year-old man straight out of university, he was mature beyond his age, possessed better judgement than many so-called experts surrounding the prime minister, and had a sense of humour I never ceased to enjoy.

So I was glad to chat with him, about the weather mostly. But, from the corner of my eye, I couldn't help but see the prime minister, some one hundred feet away, constantly looking our way when another leader was answering a question, to see what was going on. I would bet a lot that, when he went back to his suite after that, Rick was asked "what was Gratton saying?"

I can understand that it was killing him. He found out soon enough what I had to say in my book. The release came in October, while he was chairing another summit, the Commonwealth's, in Vancouver.

Somehow, through his network of contacts, Mulroney managed to get copies of the galleys of the book faxed to his suite, before the book became public at an official launch in Ottawa.

Did he read it? He swore at the time that he never had and never would—although none of his closest friends believed it. But his henchmen certainly reacted very quickly.

As had often happened in the past for other Mulroney adversaries, the job of discrediting me was given to Pat MacAdam, another crony from St. Francis Xavier University. The tall, bald Mulroney hit-man, who spoke in whispers and was as dangerous as Jack the Ripper, when it came to cutting people to pieces, was dispatched to the Canadian press room, in Vancouver.

Since, after reading the proofs of the book, they knew they couldn't attack me on the facts (as they would for Erik Nielsen, two years later), they decided to destroy my character.

MacAdam was used to this kind of dirty job. Officially, he had held the title of caucus liaison director in the PMO. But he was really the smut person, the one Mulroney used when he knew Fox, I, or others would not cooperate in character assassination. He had done a helluva job of it in the early '80s, in fact, to destroy Joe Clark and prepare Brian's re-entry.

MacAdam went to certain reporters he knew, to say basically two things: first, that I really was never told what was going on and that Mulroney didn't keep me in the know—in other words, my book was the work of an uninformed second-stringer. Secondly, that I drank too much, and spent all my evenings in Hull bars.

On the first point, anybody who can believe that I didn't know what was going on, when I spent just about every day—and sometimes night—close to the prime minister, on his plane, at public events, in his suite, is not in his right mind. If I didn't know, few people did. It was my job to know. The press didn't buy it.

The second point is more bothersome.

I was no saint. Bill Fox would have a lot of horror stories to tell about that. I'll give you just this one: on a given morning, I woke up in a strange room, with a severe hangover. It looked like a hotel room. Instinctively, I looked at the clock, thinking I had to be at work in the PMO. Horrified, I realized it was already past 10:00 a.m.. I staggered to the phone on the dresser and mechanically dialed the office number.

"Where the hell are you?" asked Fox, who, by the way, had seen his share of bad mornings in his day.

I paused, and said to him, "Wait a minute..." I put down the phone, looked out the window, saw the Ottawa River and the Parliament Buildings on the other side. Relieved, I came back to tell Fox, "I'm in Hull."

Months later, Fox was having a meeting with tour director Stewart Murray, when I called his office from out of town. Stu, who had business to do with me, asked Fox where I was.

Bill looked at him and, with typical sardonic humour, said, "Are you kidding? The last time I asked him that question, he had to put down the phone to go check out the window!"

So these things happened. I can't deny it. But I can also say that, when the coach put me on the ice, I came to play. I always did what was asked of me, and sometimes more. And there were times when the pressure of being on, seven days a week, twenty-four hours a day, got to me. So I then looked for the only kind of release I knew—a night out with my best friends. All right, some of them were women.

In any case, what burned me the most about MacAdam's accusation was that, if I did have a drinking problem, and if that was the reason for accepting my resignation, nobody ever said a word about it to me. Not the prime minister, not Bernard Roy, not Fox. And I know of other people, including a minister, who were told of such a problem when it put their careers in jeopardy.

But the word was put out.

One day, for instance, I bumped into former Ottawa mayor Lorry Greenberg, a street politician who knows just about everything that's happening in town. Greenberg and I knew each other from my City Hall reporter days. He mentioned that the word going around was that I had been let go because of my drinking. I wondered to myself, *If Brian Mulroney thought I had a problem, why did he expect me to go to the Press Club and find out what reporters were saying about him every day? If he was so concerned about my well-being, why didn't he have somebody mention it to me?*

No. That was never the problem. He didn't care if I rotted away, as long as I was useful to him. When I became a liability, I was dumped. And when I challenged him, he tried to destroy me. All in all, I suppose if you're going to take on the champion, you might as well be ready to take a few lumps.

Besides, I gave Mulroney a few good sideswipes myself, as the opposition teased him day after day, quoting passages from my book. It hurt for him, too. But an aide was to reveal to me that the revelation that hurt the most politically was when I wrote that Mulroney had deliberately delayed the CF-18 maintenance contract in the fall of 1986, to help Grant Devine's re-election as premier of Saskatchewan. The contract, when it was finally awarded to Montreal, over a better bid from Winnipeg, had Manitoba NDP Premier Howard Pawley crying foul, and caused a major federal-provincial rift. The delay in the awarding of the contract had made Winnipeg believe that it honestly had a crack at getting it. Mulroney, though, always knew it was going to Montreal's Canadair, but didn't want to hurt his Tory friend Devine's re-election plans in the neighbouring province, rightly anticipating a Western backlash over the issue. Devine won his election, defeating the NDP.

When I revealed in my book that the delay of several months had been orchestrated by Mulroney, all hell broke loose in the House of Commons and the Manitoba Legislature. Pawley still lost, and Mulroney won his re-election. But, hey, if you want to hear another one, the same prime minister delayed another important government initiative for the same premier, and for the same reasons. That was the new bill on pharmaceuticals that should have been tabled and passed in early 1986, but again was stalled because it was hurting Saskatchewan and helping Quebec.

But does it matter now?

In any case, I went through my book promotion tour for the whole month of November in a daze, rattled by the back-stabbing attempts to ruin me, and exhausted by the work itself.

It seemed that I couldn't win. Interviewers or reviewers favourable to Mulroney said I had been hard on him, while those who hated his guts, thought I had spared him. The smart ones knew I had walked a very thin tightrope between sour grapes and ass-kissing.

Luckily for me, there were a lot of these. The book was a success, but personally, I felt I had accomplished very little and was going nowhere fast.

To compound my personal problems, in February of 1988, *Le Droit* was closed down by a Typographer's Union strike. The newsroom was locked out. For me, it was a blessing in disguise. It lasted more than two months, during which time I refused to collect unemployment insurance. Not because I think it's demeaning, but because I believe the UI safety net is for workers who depend on multinational, all-powerful companies, often in remote areas, and are at the mercy of the ebbs and flows of capitalism. It is not for healthy people like myself with a specialty, who can always find work to do to support themselves.

That's how I ended up writing a few columns for a now-defunct, English-language tabloid called *The Montreal Daily News*. I didn't know it then, but that may have been the most important decision I ever made.

When the strike was over, I went back to the *Le Droit* newsroom, to find out that they really didn't want my services any more. They were cutting back staff. I remembered my previous conversation with Lacasse. At first, I was angry. How could they want to get rid of me, after pleading for me to go back less than a year earlier?

Then they offered me nine months severance pay, my second in a year. I took the money and ran...back to Parliament Hill and Brian Mulroney.

**Chapter 5**

We should have known it would only be a matter of time before Brian Mulroney called on Lucien Bouchard to do his duty and come to the rescue of The Boss.

After all, there were many who believed, during the first mandate, that Lucien had been merely "parked" out in Paris, as Canadian ambassador to France, in anticipation of the next election.

Often, when I was working in the PMO, I would hear praise showered on Bouchard, and it would almost inevitably end with the comment, "If only we had him here in Ottawa..." In fact, I probably said it myself more than once.

The dark-haired, dark-eyed Bouchard, whose Latin looks were known to make the ladies' hearts melt, was more than just another one of Mulroney's Laval University cronies. He was—in an intellectual way—the prime minister's idol.

When they were together at Laval—along with Bernard Roy and Peter White, among others—Lucien was always the first one in his law class. He was the cream of the crop and, when Lucien made an argument, about anything from a legal problem to a political plea, Mulroney would listen and look up to him. He still does.

As one aide described it to me, "His eyes still light up when Lucien speaks."

Paradoxically, however, Bouchard is just as much a fan of Brian, because the prime minister is what he never could be, a man of action. For Bouchard, Mulroney makes things happen and is truly happy only when he's at the wheel of his bulldozer. It's no accident that one of the prime minister's favorite sayings when he talks about getting back at his enemies is, "They'd better get off the track 'cause the big cars are coming!"

But Bouchard was more than just a brilliant man and loyal friend to Mulroney. He was the key to his re-election. More than that, what would happen to him in the first half of 1988 would determine whether Mulroney would call an election in the fall or wait until 1989, when his back would be to the wall.

As it turned out, the plan came very close to disaster.

✳ ✳ ✳

In his worst nightmares, Lucien Bouchard never imagined it would be like this.

Since the surprise announcement of his arrival in Ottawa, where he had been appointed Secretary of State, although unelected, on March 31, 1988, he had had ample occasion to discover the vicious side of politics.

Bouchard had been long awaited in Ottawa—and not only by the prime minister's aides. You didn't have to be much of a prophet to predict that Mulroney expected him to be part of his team for the next election campaign.

It was Mulroney's premature gamble that took everybody by surprise. The electorate doesn't take easily to ministers who are appointed to their jobs before being elected. And by-elections are never safe for government candidates, since the voters often use them to send a message to the party in power, without the risk of defeating it.

Pierre Trudeau had learned that hard lesson more than a decade earlier, when he had appointed CRTC chairman Pierre Juneau to the cabinet in the same fashion. Juneau ended up being soundly defeated by some unknown Tory, in a Montreal riding. In the Trudeau days of liberal domination in Quebec, that would normally have been unthinkable. (Juneau was later appointed chairman of the National Capital Comission and then became the head of the CBC, thanks to Pierre Trudeau.)

Was Bouchard's case different? Mulroney believed so. He thought Lucien was so popular in his hometown of Chicoutimi, on the majestic Saguenay River, that his personal appeal would outweigh any desire by the voters to dump on the government.

He may have been right...about Chicoutimi. But the plan didn't exactly unfold the way he wanted.

To understand how close Mulroney and Bouchard came to a major setback in the Lac-St-Jean riding by-election, one had to understand the politics of the region. First, this is the most nationalistic area of Quebec. It voted yes in the 1980 referendum, the only region of Quebec to do so. Lucien Bouchard was responsible for the organization of the separatist forces in his hometown—which was something the Ottawa media jumped on as soon as he stepped out of Rideau Hall, after being sworn in as a "federal" minister.

Against that background, the region of Saguenay-Lac-St-Jean is not as homogeneous as it would appear on the map.

It is a major affront to say to someone that he is from Lac-St-Jean when he's from the Saguenay, and vice-versa. The people by the big lake, and those by the river that flows from it, simply don't like each other very much.

Bouchard's hometown is on the river. That is where, ideally, he was supposed to run in the by-election.

But something went terribly wrong. Two MPs simply snubbed Mulroney.

Bernard Roy was responsible for opening up a riding for Lucien. He made the mistake of thinking that it would be easy. The first one he asked was Chicoutimi's Andre Harvey (not to be confused with Alberta's Harvie Andre.)

Not only did Harvey turn the prime minister's envoy down, he practically chastised him for wanting to take his riding away, and told him Lucien Bouchard would have to be elected at a convention if he wanted to run in Chicoutimi. He also called the local media to tell them about Roy's offer, and his intention to fight it.

Roy was beside himself. How could a backbencher defy the prime minister's authority like that? But he couldn't risk a fight with a local favourite out in the open, so he went to Plan B and asked MP Jean-Pierre Blackburn, from the neighbouring riding of Jonquiere, to relinquish his riding to Bouchard. Again, to his great astonishment, Brian's lieutenant was turned down. He asked himself if the world was going crazy. There they were, struggling to crawl back up in the polls, fresh from another scandal in Quebec (Michel Cote's resignation over an undisclosed private loan), and these MPs who had been elected on Mulroney's coat-tails in 1984 now acted like kings.

Roy was still reeling from it when he discussed it with me over lunch, a few months later.

Time quickly became Bernard Roy's enemy. If Bouchard didn't run soon, somewhere in Quebec, Mulroney risked losing the element of surprise and newness his arrival had created. With every day that passed, he was exposing himself to growing criticism about having an unelected minister in his cabinet, while Bouchard himself was being given a rough time on language issues.

Roy finally decided to cash in on an old promise. He remembered something Alma MP Clement Cote had said a few years earlier, after Mulroney's massive victory. "As I was wondering what to do, I remembered that Cote had told Lucien that, if ever he wanted to come to Ottawa, he would gladly give him his riding," Bernard told me.

He did.

I was not one to cry for Clement Cote. Not too long

before that, when I was still in Mulroney's service, he was the MP who had criticized my way of dressing, during a full caucus meeting. He had apparently said that he should ask "my wife to take him shopping."

The outburst had prompted Lac-St-Jean minister Benoit Bouchard to tell Cote, "If you don't have anything better to say, don't bother speaking."

But back to our story.

Bouchard himself had been reluctant to run in Lac-St-Jean. He knew the politics of the area well, and he had no illusions about how a boy from Chicoutimi would be perceived in Alma.

What he didn't know was that he would have to run against a man who played politics with all the ethics of a junkyard dog. The Liberals had banked on Pierre Gimael, a former Liberal MP defeated in 1984. Gimael, a descendant of Lebanese immigrants, was extremely popular in Alma. Although, in Ottawa, he was perceived as a bit of a kook by the national media, he had been effective for the riding.

Dressed like a discotheque owner, with an open collar, flashy sportcoat and gold chain, Gimael was a streetwise politician.

The Liberals couldn't have picked a better adversary for the cultured and distinguished Lucien Bouchard. Alma was not a salon of Paris, as the man the local folks derisively called "The Ambassador" would quickly found out.

Gimael went after him with wild abandon. He had nothing to lose. Bouchard and Mulroney had everything on the line.

Gimael's slogan was a thinly-veiled attempt at discrediting the Tory candidate. It said simply: La Fidelite (Fidelity). Not only did it refer silently to the fact that Bouchard had left his region to go to France (while Gimael had always been faithful to his roots), but it was also a subliminal message, reminding the local folks that Lucien had broken up with his first wife—a local girl—a few months earlier. That was also part of the Grits' whisper campaign, going door-to-door. In hindsight, the slogan was particularly ironic, given Bouchard's desertion of Mulroney just two years later.

Bouchard meanwhile, was stuck with a Tory organization that was in total disarray, and torn apart by endless in-fighting that Clement Cote had done nothing to improve.

Worse, he was a terrible politician. Those who worked on the campaign remember, for instance, how he looked when he showed up at his headquarters, ready to take part in a bicycle rally.

His advisers had told him to dress casually; in other words, not in the jacket and tie that he wore every day, like a uniform, in a blue-collar riding. Well, the organizers tried not to laugh when he showed up wearing his pin-striped suit pants and a washed-up T-shirt. Luc Lavoie convinced him that he would be the laughing stock of the town if he dared present himself in public like that. He gave Lucien other clothes to wear, but the candidate was quite insulted by the whole incident.

"Are you happy now?" he asked angrily, once he had changed.

He went to the bike rally in an awful mood and sulked the whole way. It's tough to get votes without smiling.

Sometimes, the mild-mannered Bouchard would simply explode into child-like tantrums, and complain that he'd had enough of other people telling him what to do. One of those outbursts was so comical that his good friend, Bernard Roy, had to leave the room to laugh hysterically.

In Alma, Bouchard was like a fish out of water. And he was losing. Gimael, three weeks from the election date, was eight points ahead in the polls.

Brian Mulroney sent in his shock troops.

His television guru, Luc Lavoie, a thirty-two-year-old whiz-kid and former TVA reporter on Parliament Hill, who had joined the PMO from Marcel Masse's office a few months before, landed in Alma. Lavoie, like Bouchard, was a well-cultivated man, especially for his young age.

But his heart was that of a street fighter, from his humble beginnings in the south shore city of Rimouski.

Along with Lavoie came Pierre-Claude Nolin, a long-time Tory organizer who was as hard-nosed as his six-feet-plus, 230-pound frame showed. After the 1984 campaign, he had been appointed chief-of-staff to Public Works minister Roch LaSalle, before going to the PMO to handle Quebec matters. The prime minister then made him director of the party in Quebec, when it appeared he needed a bouncer to settle some minor squabbles within the organization.

As Luc Lavoie told me about Nolin, at the time, "He's a little more of a cowboy than I am."

That said a lot. Lavoie was no choirboy himself.

For Mulroney to dispatch those two to the riding meant that the time for niceties was over.

He gave them one mission: Win. As Lavoie told me then, "First we win...Then we'll pick up the pieces."

When they got there, Bouchard was extremely depressed. He told them, "I think I have to be ready to accept defeat gracefully."

It was that bad. But Mulroney would have none of it. Defeat was unthinkable.

Word of trouble for the prestigious candidate in Alma drifted back to Ottawa, where I had just started work as a columnist for the *Montreal Daily News*.

The Toronto Economic Summit that Mulroney was to host was just weeks away. For most of the press gallery, this was the biggest event of the month. Not for me.

My knowledge of Mulroney told me that, as important as the summit was to him, his heart and mind were both a thousand kilometres away in Alma. I guessed that the bold move he had made in Lac-St-Jean was part of a greater election strategy and that, should things go Bouchard's way, the rest would unfold very quickly after that.

Consequently, I told my managing editor, Jim Duff, that the "real news" was happening in Lac-St-Jean, not in Toronto where, in any case, thousands of journalists from around the world would be watching the very predictable show on television, and all writing the same story.

I bought a plane ticket for Alma for the last weekend before Monday, June 21. That was an Air Alliance rough ride all the way—a plane I equated to a toothpaste tube with propellers. Loud ones, too.

As I was waiting in Montreal for a connecting flight, who should show up but Liberal leader John Turner and his Quebec lieutenant, MP Raymond Garneau.

Turner, whom I hardly knew at the time, treated me like an old friend. I found him a little weird, with that icy stare of his. It didn't seem to match his expressive way of talking, with his arms waving all the time.

I also thought he wore his pants funny, with the beltline resting high up under the chest. It reminded me of Big Danny, a boy I used to know at elementary school. Big Danny used to wear his pants that way, and we made fun of him.

For some strange reason, Turner wanted to discuss former Quebec Liberal premier Jean Lesage—father of the Quiet Revolution, but a long-forgotten figure since. He had always found Lesage to be such a gentleman.

He then switched to the House of Commons, and how people had no respect for each other any more. He deplored the fact that MPs could no longer have a private life.

He himself had suffered a cruel blow during an interview with CTV's Pamela Wallin, the previous January, when she had asked him if he had a drinking problem. The fact that Turner liked what he called "a little scotcherino" once in a while was no secret on Parliament Hill. I had heard stories, but I had never seen him drunk myself, nor did I have any reason to believe that the stories were not the usual inflated gossip of the Ottawa fishbowl that feeds on it.

After the Wallin interview, I wrote a column defending him in *Le Droit*. I sensed from our conversation, while waiting for the plane to Alma, that he felt he shared something with me. He alluded to the fact that I had suffered myself from the same kind of rumour-mongering in the fall of 1986, when my unfortunate adventures with two women of the press gallery had been made public.

I couldn't help but reflect, as I was talking to him, about how different Turner was from Mulroney. This man may have been a lousy politician, but he was himself. He wasn't playing a game.

Before we boarded the plane, Raymond Garneau told me that their problem in Lac-St-Jean was that the local NDP candidate, Jean Paradis, a very popular local boy, was not generating the support they had aniticipated. For Gimael to win, Paradis had to take the nationalist PQ vote away from Bouchard. But that didn't seem to be happening.

When we landed in Lac-St-Jean, Turner was confronted with the fact that Liberal premier Robert Bourassa had all but endorsed the Tory candidate in the riding—another eloquent demonstration of the love affair between him and Brian Mulroney.

It was the feisty Gimael who shot back, "If Mr. Bourassa loves Mr. Bouchard so much, why doesn't he call him to sit in Quebec City?"

I drove into town with Heather Bird, an Ottawa correspondent then with *The Toronto Star*, who had been intensely studying French in Jonquiere for a few weeks, and living with a unilingual family.

She was driving the car, but one of the sons of the family was giving the directions...in French. It was interesting for me, sitting in the back seat, to experience bilingual Canada at work.

Heather, who later came to *The Ottawa Sun*, kept getting confused with the word *droit*, which normally means "right" in French—as in "turn right." Except that, when you say *tout droit*, it means "go straight."

Well, by the time she was finished, I wasn't sure what was left, right, forward or backward myself. I told Heather that maybe she shouldn't speak French and drive at the same time.

It was a nice tour of the riding, though.

As soon as I unloaded my bags at the hotel, I headed for the most famous landmark in Alma, the Mario Tremblay Brasserie. Mulroney had been there a week before, while campaigning in the riding with Bouchard.

The Tories had arranged for former Canadiens hockey star Mario Tremblay—now a radio sports reporter—to fly down to his hometown and bar to accompany the prime minister on his visit.

It was a shrewd move. Since Mario was coming to meet the prime minister, the expense of flying there did not have to be computed as a campaign expense. The meter would start ticking only when Brian's car crossed the boundary line of the riding. But that was not the only deception in this campaign event that got Mulroney and his pony a lot of publicity, both locally and provincially.

That same night, I went out to dinner with the Tory organizers, among them one of the PM's boys, Pierre-Claude Nolin. As we discussed the campaign, the subject drifted to Mario Tremblay and the brasserie he owned there.

"He doesn't own it," said a local organizer, who was a Bourasssa Liberal at the provincial level. "He sold it a couple of years ago."

Pierre-Claude Nolin was stone-faced, as I looked sideways at him.

"What do you mean he doesn't own it?" I asked incredulously.

"He sold it to his best friend. Mario hardly ever comes here anymore."

We'd been had.

To the national media, Mario Tremblay had greeted Brian Mulroney and Lucien Bouchard in his domain, when he had flown in from Montreal for the momentous occasion. But it was as fake as a Hollywood backdrop. It bore his name, all right, but it wasn't his. Tremblay had been born and raised there, but he didn't even bother coming any more.

Quite a con job, to sell a candidate who was trying to picture himself as Mr. Clean.

To help promote this immaculate image, Bouchard had introduced, for the first time in a federal election campaign, a method of raising money known as "popular fund-raising," which basically excluded corporate donations. It was an idea he had borrowed from Rene Levesque's PQ, which actually passed in Quebec the toughest electoral financing law in the country, virtually eliminating the possibility, or the appearance, of kickbacks.

Bouchard's fund-raising campaign was extremely successful in Lac-St-Jean. But, while he was playing that "pure" card, behind him, Mulroney's capos were devising ways of making millions of dollars in subsidies rain on the riding. Regional files that had been stuck in Ottawa's red-tape for months, even years, suddenly were mysteriously unlocked. The people of Lac-St-Jean started to understand the meaning of power—and that's exactly what Brian Mulroney wanted.

Against that background, the Mario Tremblay Brasserie coup was small potatoes. At least it didn't cost the taxpayers any money.

But, as much as Lucien Bouchard had wanted to picture himself as the man who would bring honesty and integrity back to the regime, this by-election was a perfect example of how far Brian Mulroney was willing to go to get what he wanted. Anything goes, as long as it is within the confines of the law.

If Lucien's innocence had to be sacrificed in the process, so be it. Win first. Apologize later.

During the last two weeks of the campaign, Mulroney was on the phone every day to his boys and Lucien, urging them on like a general. He wanted to know every detail of everything that was going on.

When he flew down to the riding himself, a little more than a week before the election, it was to show Lucien how it was done. And it was easy to spot the real politician, when they visited a farm together. Mulroney was dressed casually in a short-sleeved shirt, while stuffy Lucien had to take off his jacket and loosen his tie to look almost relaxed amid the cows and flies.

Although he never said it, I'm sure Mulroney enjoyed every minute of the lesson he had just served his neophyte politician.

As I learned about all this, on the weekend that preceded the by-election, I shrugged. Nothing I could do or write now could change the outcome. The prime minister's commandos had turned it around for Lucien, and the election was in the bag.

So, on the Saturday night before voting day, I went to the hotel's discotheque. I was fascinated to find out that, in Alma, when people want to insult one another, they call them "welfares."

And who should show up but an ebullient Lucien Bouchard. The man had suddenly become a politician, shaking hands and kissing girls, now that he knew he was winning.

He invited me to sit beside him.

"Looks like you're gonna win," I said.

"I think so," he said gravely, "but he made us sweat!" He was referring to his true-grit adversary, Gimael.

On election day, the prime minister was in Toronto, hosting the Economic Summit. But, somehow, he managed to have his executive assistant phone the riding just about every hour on the hour, to make sure "the boys bring out the vote."

As the early returns came in shortly after eight o'clock, showing that his pony had come in by several lengths, Mulroney put on his dinner jacket and told his aides solemnly, "You know, this is only a by-election. I have to take care of the affairs of state."

He was serious. The man who had been obsessed with Lucien's election for months, now tried to act as if it had never mattered all that much to him. Even his aides—used to his theatrics—were shell-shocked.

He then went to a working dinner at the University of Toronto's Hart House, with the six most powerful leaders of the Western World.

Britain's Margaret Thatcher went over to him and asked, "Brian, did we win?"

**Chapter 6**

I guess I just have a way of getting in trouble with the man.

It certainly didn't take long to happen, in the summer of 1988. I had barely gotten back on Parliament Hill, and already my former boss and I were crossing swords.

The first time it happened wasn't so bad; it was more aggravating than anything else. The second incident, however, had the prime minister of the country considering making a little voodoo doll in my image.

I may, in fact, have been looking for trouble the first time, when I decided to accompany him on a visit to his riding. Press advance man Jacques Labrie—whom I had hired in the PMO—couldn't believe his ears, when I told him on the phone that I would like to be part of the press corps for the quick visit to Sept-Iles in August.

"Holy shit!" was about the only comment he could come up with.

You have to remember, of course, that at that time, Brian Mulroney couldn't even bear to hear my name. In fact, he had specifically banned my columns from his daily clippings.

One day, an over-zealous aide let one of my columns slip. He thought the prime minister would enjoy reading it, since it was rather favourable.

Well, Mulroney got on the phone to the press office as soon as he laid eyes on my black and white face. "You guys laughing at me?" he asked a stunned press secretary. "I told you I didn't want him in there."

One other columnist was also on that blacklist. But he had been for a long time. That was Claire Hoy, then of *The Toronto Sun*. When I was told the story by one of my buddies within the government, I couldn't help but smile at the fact that Hoy and I were now in the same boat. How things change. And I didn't know it then, but the future would be even weirder.

So, as I boarded the chartered press plane to Sept-Iles and Baie Comeau, I had some mixed feelings about being face to face with Brian Mulroney again. It would, in fact, be the first time I had seen him up close since Bill Fox's fortieth birthday party, a year earlier, when he had learned of my writing a book. He hadn't even looked at me then, and I certainly wasn't expecting a warmer reception this time.

I put on a brave front for the boys, though, as my fellow reporters kept ribbing me about whether I intended to scrum the prime minister or not. I laughed at such a prospect, but I really was terrified inside.

However, the other side of it was that I really liked going to the riding of Manicouagan. The Sept-Iles fresh shrimp and crab were well worth the trip, especially considering that somebody else was paying for the ticket—the same price as a trip to Paris.

We were also expecting news to break out, since the prime minister was on the verge of calling an election. It was doubtful that he would do that while visiting Manicouagan, but he seemed to be taking pleasure in dropping hints about it here and there. In a pre-election atmosphere, every word that the man with the power utters can take on incredible proportions.

In any case, with the rest of the press gallery ruffians, I got on the plane, a turbo-prop Convair that travelled separately from Mulroney, and took almost twice the time to get to the North Shore city, sixteen hundred kilometres away. (When he travels inside the country, the prime minister uses the small Challenger jet that, at maximum capacity, seats twelve people; the last people he'd want on there with him are members of the media. He can barely stand some members of his own staff. Internationally, he usually travels on an Armed Forces Boeing 707 with the media at the back of the plane.)

There wasn't much to report until Mulroney delivered what was to be his last speech as MP for the town of Sept-Iles. Because, although he didn't say it at the time, he had already decided by then that, thanks to a modified electoral map, he would be running in the neighbouring riding of Charlevoix. That more prosperous and problem-free region included his hometown of Baie Comeau. All he had to do to get it was bump out local Tory MP Charles Hamelin—something relatively easy for a prime minister to do.

Once in Charlevoix, Mulroney wouldn't have to worry about the horrendous promises he had to make to the economically depressed area of Sept-Iles and Port-Cartier. The most controversial of his mandate, of course, had been the building of the Port-Cartier maximum security prison—but other millions had been showered on the riding over the previous four years. The national media would periodically underline this "convenient" spending of taxpayers money in Manicouagan while, in the local press, Mulroney was being criticized for not doing enough.

The problem with the national press was, in my view, two-fold. First, there usually wasn't much news to justify a rather expensive outing, and telling your desk about another Mulroney promise to his folks sold well. Secondly, as much as Mulroney said his government intended to help all remote areas of the country, such as Manicouagan, he never seemed to back up his claim with any concrete evidence. Where were the other prisons, the other roads?

That was something I had mentioned to him myself,

while I was in the PMO. On one trip, when he had asked me what the boys were saying, I had told him worriedly that, although his promises played well in the riding, the national media would inevitably exploit them as a major patronage effort.

He had answered defiantly, "Let them do it! Good!"

There was little point in reasoning with him when he reacted that way.

And now, from the other, safer, side of the fence, as I listened to his last Sept-Iles speech, on that August day of 1988, I shook my head in disbelief. The stubborn man was doing it again. Weeks away from an election, he gave a list of every major million-dollar project he had obtained for the riding of Manicouagan, and then upped the ante by promising the imminent building of a $1.4 billion aluminium smelter in the area.

At the back of the room, the scribes from the national media smiled. Then they scrummed him, and asked about how many millions in subsidies his government had given to his riding. He said, angrily, that he didn't have the answer handy.

That, of course, was not true. If he didn't have it handy, there was no doubt that his riding assistant and longtime supporter, Keith Morgan, knew of every cent that had been spent and where it had gone. Morgan, like his son Rick after him, was too efficient not to know. His briefing books were always the best in the PMO.

At that point I just chuckled. No wonder, I told myself, we'd had so many problems. How could anybody seriously believe Mulroney didn't know the figures, when he had just delivered a speech boasting about it all?

I wrote about it in *The Montreal Daily News*, and I'm sure Mulroney didn't appreciate it too much.

But it was what I found out later in the trip that really provoked his anger.

At first, I was quite surprised at the friendliness of his entourage toward me. The only one who seemed to avoid me consciously was Brian's brother, Bill, who had also acted as his representative in the riding. I understood that because, although Bill looked a lot like a shorter version of his brother, he was not at all like Brian when it came to confrontational politics and need for public attention.

He was a mild-mannered, soft-spoken man, extremely sensitive to media criticism, in an almost boyish sort of way. He just couldn't understand why journalists were so nasty. When we worked together in Manicouagan, we used to get along famously, but he told me more than once, "You're a nice guy. How could you have ever been one of those bastards?"

I laughed. And I felt bad when I saw him in Sept-Iles, scurrying away from the media (not just me), because I figured he must think by now that I was a bastard too.

But other Mulroney aides were suprisingly friendly and open. To my great surprise, one of them came up to me and started spilling the beans about what was going on in the PMO, with the election looming. That person told me how Ontario's Big Blue Machine heavies, headed by Senator Norm Atkins, were muscling in on the prime minister's staff, to grab the prestigious campaign jobs.

When I found out that even faithful Stewart Murray was being shoved aside and treated like dirt, I didn't need any more to fill my acid pen. Murray, a slim, bespectacled former rocker who now looked like a choir boy, was, over the years, the most loyal foot-soldier Mulroney had. His wife and family hardly ever saw him, as he was gone on advance trips around the country, and the world, most of the year. He probably took better care of the Mulroney kids than he did his own. He also knew the system, what The Boss needed and wanted and, more importantly, what he didn't like. And he had stuck with it for four years, believing that, when the election came along, he would be there to battle alongside the prime minister.

I knew how important going through the election campaign was to Murray. We had discussed it before, when I had talked about leaving the PMO. It would be his crowning achievement. Now that he had come so far, through sometimes perilous waters, the Big Blue guys were trying to push him aside as some amateurish valet who knew nothing about an election tour.

The guy was my friend, and I didn't have too many of those in the Big Blue. Stu and I had been through a lot together. The Big Blue had put us through a lot. I had a legitimate chance to kick back.

So I waited until we got back to Ottawa to break the story. Had I done so during the trip itself, Mulroney would have launched a major investigation to find out which one of his aides had dared to even look at me—never mind tell me what was going on inside his office.

I wrote a story about how the PMO was in shambles, as a result of the Big Blue's tactics and that, on the eve of the election, nobody knew who was going to do what during the campaign—more specifically on the campaign plane.

Although I didn't single him out, chief Tory organizer Harry Near was furious, and quickly got on the phone to other media to deny the story.

But on Parliament Hill, veteran reporters were ready to buy my story, knowing that I wouldn't write something about my former colleagues without being damn sure of my sources. It may have been the story in fact, that made some of them realize how valuable an ally I had become.

It was also a painful reminder to Mulroney himself of how annoying I could be on the other side of the fence. He found out that same afternoon.

As he left the Commons Question Period to climb the stairs up to his second-floor office, reporter Bob Fife shouted a question—the way the media pack always does, in the hope that Boss Brian will deign to pay attention to them.

"How is your campaign organization, Prime Minister?" asked Fife.

Mulroney gave him his iciest of stares and said disdainfully, "Are there any other questions?"

Edison Stewart of Canadian Press (now of *The Toronto Star*), another one of Mulroney's "favourite" boys, followed up with, "How is your campaign organization, Prime Minister?"

White with rage, Mulroney turned on his heel and stormed up to his office. All the while, he could hear the laughs and hollers of the amused media behind him.

He must have just loved me then.

The second embarrassing encounter I had with him, in the summer of my return to political journalism, was a little more serious.

That time, it was I who had opened my big mouth a little too wide.

*"So, What Are the Boys Saying?"* had just come out in paperback. The publisher was hoping to cash in on the awaited election campaign. They sent me on a short promotion tour that took me to Toronto, and a lunch with *Globe and Mail* columnist and author of the bestselling book, *Ottawa Inside Out*, Stevie Cameron.

Cameron told me she didn't even know if she was going to write anything out of our conversation. I didn't mind. It was nice to just talk casually for a change, instead of being assaulted by the same old questions.

So I guess I started babbling away a little.

We were discussing the story she had broken the previous year, about the extensive renovations at 24 Sussex, and the Mulroneys' taste for luxury. I let her know that the story had not made her too popular with Canada's first couple.

Stevie confided in me that she had felt harassed and taken aback by the personal attacks launched against her after that, and was genuinely surprised at the wrath she had unleashed in Mulroney.

I let her know I wasn't surprised; that it had always been that way. Many times I had tried to make the prime minister understand that those petty stories didn't matter very much. I used to compare it to Trudeau, who just shrugged that kind of stuff off.

"Mulroney still doesn't understand that the more he lets it be known that it bothers him, the more he exposes himself to that kind of stuff," I said.

I also told Cameron about how difficult they had

made things for me, because I had written the book. Even then, though, I didn't go into the details of it. But when she asked me if I thought Brian Mulroney was a good prime minister I answered, "My honest opinion is that Brian Mulroney is a good prime minister. But he's got this vindictive side to him that is dangerous, that will blow up in his face some day. He's a bully."

The pitch was out of my hands, and the home run was out of the park.

Cameron reported the comments a few days later in a column. The *Globe* made my words the "Quote of the Day" on the front page.

As usual, it looked a lot worse in black and white than it sounded coming out of my mouth. I certainly couldn't deny that I had said it, nor that I surely meant it at the time.

The first one of Mulroney's boys to phone me was Luc Lavoie, then in charge of breaking in Lucien Bouchard to Ottawa's back-stabbing world.

"I guess he's pissed off," I said.

"It's not only that...he's deeply hurt, deeply hurt," he said.

I felt bad. Maybe I had gone a little too far. Maybe it was fine to feel that way in private and share my thoughts with my closest friends, but to tell a reporter...

I didn't back down and pretend I hadn't said it, however. I didn't even pull it out of context. I just said I hadn't specifically demanded an interview with Stevie Cameron to tell her how much of a bully Brian Mulroney was.

The next one to call was Bill Fox. He wanted to have lunch at the Four Seasons. I agreed.

He didn't have to tell me what it was about. I felt bad for Fox, too. He still considered himself responsible for me and whatever I had done, since it had been his idea to put me on Mulroney's team in the first place. Whenever I'd get out of line, he'd be the first one to be hit with the line, "And you hired that asshole!"

Fox really wanted to know why on earth I had said

what I was quoted as saying. I told him the story of how Peter White had suggested I be fired from *Le Droit* a year earlier.

He was stunned. I knew Fox well, and I hadn't seen that look on his face too often. He was usually prepared for the worst revelation.

He simply said, "I didn't know that." He never said he didn't believe it. Then he added, nodding his head, "Well, if that's the way it's going to be..."

Typically, his sense of honour and fair play had taken over from his loyalty to The Boss. If we two wanted to fight it out to the end, that was fine with him.

But Mulroney also sent me a message himself. Through the months that followed the publication of the book, he deliberately restrained himself from commenting on it. Even when the opposition would quote from it and mention my name in Question Period, he'd act as if he'd never heard of me. But this time was too much.

During an interview with *Toronto Star* columnist Carol Goar, he said something I'm sure was intended for me.

Goar's story was designed to give the human side of Brian Mulroney's cardboard figure. What we call a "fluff" piece, the kind that are nice to read once in a while. As with everything else concerning The Boss, I couldn't help reading it.

And there it was, between quotation marks, the cryptic message to traitor Michel.

Mulroney was talking about how Mila was a lot better at accepting criticism than he was. He gave an example of someone breaking a confidence about them. He was upset, but Mila told him not to take it personally; that the person was just trying to earn a living. Now, there weren't too many people at the time who were trying to earn a living by "breaking confidences" involving Brian Mulroney.

When I told Fox about it, he chuckled and said, in his laconic style, "Nope...there aren't too many who fit the description."

The whole thing didn't go any further. The election was simply too close for either of us to get into an even dirtier public spat.

Besides, my editor at the *Daily News*, Jim Duff, had already accepted my campaign coverage plan, which meant I would have to travel extensively on the candidates' planes—including three weeks with Mulroney. I believed that an election was the best kind of drama in politics, because it had a beginning and an end. To make the drama live, you needed actors, and those were the leaders. He bought it.

I let a few of the Hill boys know that I would be on "the plane." It didn't take long for another one of Mulroney's staffers, speech writer and former *Le Droit* colleague Paul Terrien, to ask me, "Are you going on the plane?"

"Yes."

"Mulroney's plane?"

"Yes."

"Holy shit..."

*This is a very shabby book, both in subject and in style.*

# Chapter 7

**T**rying not to be seen, Mila whispered something in Brian's ear.

I didn't hear what she said. I didn't have to. I'd heard the cue many times before. "Turn around and wave."

Like the President and the First Lady, the Queen and the Prince, Canada's Ken and Barbie wheeled around like a pair of dancers at the top of the airplane ramp and, just before crossing the open door, smiled their perfect smiles and waved regally to the small crowd of Tiny Tories who had come to say goodbye at Ottawa's Uplands airport.

I smiled too. I'd seen the move rehearsed so many times. They were darn good at it, I told myself, looking from the other side now.

I remembered also how Mila had perfected the way to wave through an airplane window, trying to show her husband. It was an unnatural kind of wave, with the hand doing a short, mechanical, chopping motion, but for the people outside, it looked absolutely real.

This would be the picture in the newspapers tomorrow.

The photo opportunity done with, Brian and Mila engulfed themselves into what would be their home for the next fifty days—the plane.

In modern election campaigns, it has taken on mythical proportions. When somebody asks, "Are you going to be on the plane?" it's like asking if you've got an invitation to heaven. This is true both for journalists—especially the younger ones—and for political staffers.

It's even more crucial to the latter, because proximity to The Boss creates the illusion that you are important and influential. That, of course, is a mirage. Brian Mulroney will listen to you when—and only when—he chooses to, whether you're standing a metre from him or you're at the end of the phone, a thousand kilometres away. Bernard Roy, for instance, rarely travelled with the prime minister, yet he was one of the most influential persons around him.

Under Mulroney's direct guidance, and with lots of cash, the Tories have perfected the campaign plane. Their aircraft, since the 1984 campaign, is by far the most efficient election machine of all three parties, in terms of both available space and the leader's privacy.

First of all, it's a Boeing 727. That model was preferred to the smaller DC-9 by Mulroney's team in 1984, and they repeated four years later. The Liberals, who had heard and read all about how superior the Tory plane had been to theirs, also tried to get a 727 from Air Canada in 1988. But the company's Hugh Riopel had to tell them there weren't enough 727s in the fleet to accomodate more than one party—and the governing party had the first choice. However, Riopel, arguably the most effective PR man of the last decade on Parliament Hill—a man who managed to be a personal friend to both Don Mazankowski and Jean Chretien had to be—manoeuvred to get Canadian into the deal. The Liberals ended up with a Boeing 737, which was an improvement on the DC-9. The NDP stuck to the old plane, since a deal with First Air fell through. So the Mulroney aircraft, in terms of slickness and efficiency, was still tops.

First there was the added space. Not only did it allow Mulroney and his top aides to be isolated from the media riff-raff, in a protective cocoon with first-class seating at the front of the plane—where working tables were also set up—but it also provided more space for the steadily-growing travelling media. Which kept "the boys" happy.

(I still call the media "the boys," because that's how Mulroney used to refer to them when I was at his side. But, in fact, during the 1988 campaign, for some perverse reason, he chose to call them, in French, "our little kittens." He would regularly ask his aides with some derision, "So, are our little kittens happy?")

But the second most important feature of the 727 for Mulroney was the fact that it had two doors, one at the front and another one at the back of the aircraft. This meant that the candidate could enter and exit his cubicle at the front without having to mix with the media ruffi-ans, armed with their cameras, tape-recorders and big mouths. They entered and exited through the back door.

In the first days of the 1988 campaign, Mulroney's team refined the technique even more, in a way that drew ridicule from the media. At nearly every campaign stop—including the deboarding of the airplane—they would have local volunteers install chains, behind which the media scrummers were expected to docilely stand. Needless to say the little kittens were quite agitated by the whole thing.

They also had a little fun with it. Sometimes the chains would have to be held up by volunteers—at an airport, for instance, where the regulations didn't allow the installation of fences on the tarmac before the arrival of the aircraft. At one of those stops, the media rowdies, spotting the chains held up by human posts, told the impressionable volunteers that they were expected to keep moving to the right as the media advanced. They obeyed the order. As a result, you had a twenty-foot chain running around the tarmac of an airport.

The technique actually earned the Mulroney team the nickname of "The Chain Gang." CBC veteran cameraman

Gerry Beauchamp—a former disc jockey known as "The Doctor," who provided the musical entertainment on the plane throughout the campaign—had special T-shirts made with "Chain Gang" emblazoned on the front and Mulroney's immortal words, "That's what it's all about" on the back. They went like hotcakes.

But Mulroney's attempts at controlling the media weren't all funny. His use of a huge RCMP bodyguard corps to shield him from the media came very close to turning the police into a political force.

But more on that a little later. Back to that first take-off from Ottawa.

I felt weird, sitting at the back of the plane, wearing jeans and a leather jacket. Weird and strangely happy.

I remembered Mulroney's words to Bill Fox, during the first election campaign. "Would you like to be sitting with those guys at the back of the plane?" he had asked mockingly, meaning that power was a far greater rush than taking notes on what the powerful—like himself—said.

The thought made me smile. *Yes, you're damned right I'm happier here*, I would have liked to tell him. But he probably would have thought I was lying.

Most of the faces at the front of the plane were those of friends; people who, over the last year or so, had either been avoiding me or been very careful about being seen in public with me. Some of them, I had hired. Quite a few had actually been working under me in the Press Office.

Now I was the enemy. It wasn't going to be easy for either of us. I knew what I was doing, though. But I'm not sure they knew who they were dealing with.

After the story I had written a few weeks earlier about the Big Blue Machine muscling in on the PM's staff, it was nice to see that most of his key people had made the plane, although the tour manager, technically the plane's chief-of-staff, was a product of the Big Blue; John Tory, a bright young Bill Davis protege with a pre-destined name.

The original plan called for a co-tour manager, to take

over in Quebec, where the unilingual John Tory might encounter some communications problems. But I suspect I scuttled that one.

Gary Ouellet, an Ottawa lobbyist with the powerful GCI (Government Consultants International) firm—of Frank Moores fame—and a friend of Mulroney's, was slated for the job. But the problem was that Ouellet's firm held a lucrative lobbying contract at the time with the British builders of the Trafalgar-class nuclear submarine Canada was considering buying. The British were locked in a fierce battle with the French Amethyste submarine that seemed to have won the favour of the military. Companies don't mess around with $5 billion government contracts. They don't shoot each other, but almost.

I had written a column in August about the fact that lobbyist Gary Ouellet would be "tucking the prime minister into bed every night" during the campaign, and linked his firm to the British submarine bid. The PMO's Luc Lavoie had phoned me afterward and casually asked if that was really all that important.

"Important!" I said, disbelievingly, knowing Lavoie's flair for a news story. "The nuclear submarines will be an issue in the campaign, the contract is not awarded yet and a GCI lobbyist will be sitting at the front of the plane with Mulroney. You ask me if it's important! I'll tell you what, if the media don't jump on it, the French Amethyste group certainly will."

Ouellet didn't make the plane, and budget cuts later sank the subs that never surfaced.

But John Tory, in the end, turned out to be an excellent manager, who earned the respect of an initially slightly hostile PMO staff that saw him as an outsider.

The mood was upbeat, but quietly so, as the plane took off at around 9:30 on that sunny October morning, two days after Mulroney's dramatic election call at Government House.

The Mulroney people, like The Boss, are a serious bunch on the road. They're working. It's not that they wouldn't enjoy hamming it up a little, but the head man would not be amused.

In fact, two of his aides got "caught" by the principal drinking wine with their meal on the plane, at the end of a hard day. Mulroney innocently called both Luc Lavoie, his TV expert, and Marc Lortie, my successor as press secretary, and told them he didn't appreciate them falling off the wagon so wildly.

"You know, I used to drink wine, boys," he told the two grown men. "I probably drank more wine in my life than the both of you ever will together. Now I don't drink any more. When you drink, you make mistakes." And he gave examples of people in politics who had made mistakes for that reason.

Lavoie and Lortie were stunned. They weren't exactly over-indulging. Both of them loved a party, but neither one was a heavy drinker.

Mulroney really didn't mess around. In 1984, when I was at the front of the plane, it hadn't been that severe. A lot of the staffers had personally decided to take what they called "The Pledge" not to drink for the seven weeks of the election campaign. But it was a personal decision, which had been brought on more by the example provided by The Boss than by his direct order. I was not one of those. Quite the contrary, I was expected to have a drink with "the boys."

But, in 1988, maybe even "the boys" had really become kittens and preferred milk to suds. The parties—the all-nighters we used to have during the roaring '70s campaigns—had all but disappeared...Nah! Not quite. Some of us still managed to abuse and enjoy ourselves. But we—yes, you'll be surprised to know I was one of those—were in the minority.

The media's new clean and sober attitude is partly a direct result of the new Perrier morality that has engulfed the Western World, including journalism, and partly attributable to a changing business—especially on the electronic side—where TV, for instance, has almost as many news bulletins daily as radio networks. This, of course, puts even more pressure on radio reporters. I like to kid them about their relative unimportance in the public information process, but I must say that, during the 1988 campaign in particular, I was amazed at the amount of work these men and women had to do in the course of a day. They never seemed to stop.

The "scrum" phenomenon has also taken over the print media. It seems that a campaign day is not newsworthy if the media don't get a crack at screaming provocative questions at the candidate. Just covering the event is seldom good enough.

Some, like *The Toronto Star*'s excellent political reporter, Linda Diebel, genuinely felt guilty about it. On the third day of Mulroney's well-controlled campaign, she started agitating with her media colleagues that we had to scrum. "We can't let them get away with this," she said, at another photo opportunity in Saskatchewan. Her next comment was, "What do we ask him?"

Diebel, a blonde sparkplug of a woman with an incisive pen, was also the one who pointed out to me, as the plane took off on the first day, that she'd read somewhere that Mulroney had called me "a rogue elephant."

I didn't know what that meant, but it sure sounded funny. Diebel said, giggling, that she thought it had something to do with virility. The *Sun*'s Tim Naumetz explained that it was a lone elephant that went around trampling people. All right. But what did that have to do with me?

I asked press secretary Marc Lortie about it. He chuckled and told me later in a whisper, still chuckling, "I checked with The Boss. He says he never used that expression."

I'm sure the ones he did use were less flattering.

It wasn't all laughs, however. As I pointed out earlier in this chapter, some of Mulroney's handlers set out deliberately, at the beginning of the campaign, to use the RCMP VIP bodyguards to protect the prime minister from the press. That was a clear abuse of power on the part of the PMO, and the officers who were asked to do it told me over a beer that they weren't thrilled at all.

I couldn't help thinking of how Bill Fox would have shivered at the thought of such police intervention.

While he was Press Secretary, during the 1984 campaign, he was adamantly opposed to any intervention on the part of the police force with the media. He dealt with them. When I succeeded him, I simply followed what was, to me, normal procedure.

In fairness, though, the Mounties had been broken into such a media-control role during the Trudeau days, when they were extensively used in that fashion.

To be perfectly honest, while I was a press secretary, there were many times when I would have loved to be in the same situation as the American White House press guys. They didn't have to worry about hand-to-hand combat between the president and the media. The assassination attempt on Ronald Reagan—where John Hinckley had hidden among a group of reporters, to shoot at the president from a short distance—had solved that problem. Even the American media were now part of the crowd-control strategy.

"Crowd control," in fact, was the PMO's magic term to describe the use of an inordinate number of Mounties during that first week of the campaign. They thought they had a good excuse, since an incident the previous spring in Moncton, New Brunswick, when Mila had been injured while she, the prime minister, and their police escort were going through a crowd of demonstrators. But I knew that the Moncton incident had simply been the result of sloppy work on the part of the PMO's second-string advance team and the local RCMP detachment. I knew the "crowd control" excuse couldn't stand up to the facts.

From day one, there were confrontations and shouting matches between the RCMP and the media on Mulroney's plane. Deliberately, I didn't get involved. I felt I was still too close to my former incarnation in the PMO to start telling people to do things the way I would have done them. Even from a distance, I didn't miss anything. It was evident to me that orders had been given. But my cup overflowed in Calgary, on the second day of the campaign, when Mulroney held a press conference in a hotel meeting room. It wasn't what he had to say at the press conference that bothered me. It was what happened after.

Picture this: present in a private hotel meeting-room were the prime minister and his handlers, the media and several RCMP bodyguards—more than ten, for sure. Nobody from the public. No crowd to control.

The media obediently stood behind the ropes, a safe distance away from the prime minister.

But when the press conference ended, the Mounties, who were between the media and the door through which Mulroney was exiting, stood in a row, side by side, and locked arms like riot police.

What for? Even the media weren't moving. Everybody had already had his or her "clip." Nobody was going to chase down the prime minister. And, if they had, what did that have to do with his physical safety?

I was stunned that they would do something that stupid. I looked incredulously at Luc Lavoie, standing on the other side of the Mountie front line, and said in a loud voice, "This is what you call crowd control?"

Luc just stared at me. He knew it was a mistake.

That same night, I had a few beers with a couple of RCMP VIP officers and I told them what was on my mind. "Well, I'm glad to talk finally to somebody who understands," one of them told me. They didn't like what they were being asked to do any more than we did.

The next day, I wrote a story about it. When asked about my story, the PM's spokesman, Marc Lortie, did the smart thing. He said I had been absolutely right and that things would change. The police seemed to fade away from the media's path, although they would still be called upon to help out when a camera crew, for instance, was in a location the PM's handlers didn't like.

However, two years later, in a private conversation with another RCMP officer who had played an active part in the campaign, I learned something about their role that even I would never have dreamed possible at the time.

The man, who has to remain anonymous, told me that I had been specifically targeted by some of

Mulroney's aides. "They told us to watch you in scrums and public events more than anybody else. After watching you operate for a few days, I couldn't understand what they were talking about," he said. "You seemed like a very reasonable and nice guy. And most of the time, you'd be standing away from where the action was, around the prime minister. I couldn't figure out what they were so afraid of."

I was so flabbergasted that I asked him if he was kidding. He said he wasn't, but he didn't tell who, in the organization, gave the order. Whoever it was, if the order was given by anyone, that person had to be taking a cue from what was being said about me higher up. I still shake my head in disbelief at their stupidity. As if the PM couldn't have handled me himself. They were afraid of their own shadows.

But, as important as that may have been, the involvement and abusive use of the RCMP was just a sideshow to the main event.

The pace of the Mulroney campaign in those first two weeks was staggering, but predictable. A photo opportunity in the morning for the pretty pictures, a speech at noon for "content," and a partisan crowd in the evening to pump up the troops.

Three events a day is not exactly back-breaking. But this campaign had a new twist, apart from the chain gang—some pseudo-brilliant plan the Tory strategists had come up with in their spare time. Instead of sleeping in the town where we held our last event—as candidates had done for the previous century—the plane would take off after the reporters' filing time was over, and high-tail it out of town, en route to its next destination. As a result, we would arrive at our hotels half conked, in the middle of the night. There we would head for the so-called "hospitality suite," which is a polite term, borrowed from political conventions, that means there's free beer on the menu. That's all you need at 3:00 a.m., after a long flight. But we took it in stride, since we had little choice; once booked at the hotel, we still had to wait for our luggage to arrive.

After a couple of days of this crazy schedule, I asked
Stu Murray what the hell they had in mind, putting us
to bed as the sun came up. He explained that it was part
of a new strategy; that the Tories preferred to sleep
where the morning's event was to happen, instead of flying early to the destination. With November looming, a
freak snow storm was always possible.

Nevertheless, I was enjoying myself like a kid at
Disneyland. This was so easy and so much fun compared
to the front of the plane. Now I could laugh and make
jokes at Mulroney too. And I didn't have to hide to do it.
I could even complain about the travel accomodations.

This was the life, and I took in the scenery with a certain inner serenity.

On the first day, we went to a place called
Georgetown, north of Toronto, to a factory named Mold-
Masters. They made plastic molds, and one of their
products was called a "Big Shot." They advertised it as
"A Big Shot for big parts." The boys on the bus got a kick
out of that.

Two days later, I couldn't help thinking of the "Big
Shot" when we went to Prince George, B.C. The northern town has a mascot they call Mister P.G. (pronounced
peegee). The towering, forty-foot statue of a lumberjack
with a hard hat greets you as you come into town. It
used to be made of B.C. timber; now it's plastic.

Mister P.G. has another claim to fame. Every
Hallowe'en, local high school students pull a prank on
the mascot that very often has sexual connotations. That
year, the pranksters decided that Mister P.G., in the
AIDS era, had to set a good example and practice safe
sex. So they stuck a huge piece of timber between the
mascot's legs, as they had done in the past. But this
time, they covered it with a parachute.

The next day, I really started to suspect that the subliminal message in Mulroney's campaign was a sexual
one, when we ended up on a farm in the middle of
nowhere, somewhere south of Saskatoon.

That's where we were introduced to Thor, a big,
mean, black bull, our photo op of the day. Thor didn't

know it, but he was a major part of Brian Mulroney's reelection hopes.

Thor's job was to make babies, about a hundred calves a year. He was worth about $100,000, though some said he could go for as much as $350,000. (We know what you are Thor; we're just negotiating your price.)

Brian showed up to see the bull in his Guccis, while Mila, dressed all in green, like a blade of grass, was wearing kid gloves of the same colour. There is still a legend going around that somehow Thor's urge to make babies started to grow as Mila approached. Well, I was there and, if that's all Thor has to show, his reputation is a lot of bull.

With all the fun, though, one thing was starting to get to me—the food. Sandwiches and popcorn on the bus and airplane microwave specials get to you after a while.

So far, the best meal we thought we would have, had miserably backfired on the bus from Calgary to Red Deer—a good two-hour drive—on the second day of the campaign. We had been promised pizza and, like a bunch of kids, we were all looking forward to it.

It was easy to eat and work on the Tories' modern buses, which were all equipped with several tables, as well as a fridge for the beer and Perrier and a microwave oven for the popcorn.

I was the first one to reach the pizza boxes. I opened the first one. "Hawaiian pizza?" I cringed, spotting the pieces of pineapple on top of the Mozarella cheese.

"Yuk!" went the bus. I opened the second box, the third, the fourth...All Hawaiian pizza.

"Who the fuck ordered this?" I screamed.

The bus driver—one of our three regulars—said it must have been the driver from the other vehicle. "He likes Hawaiian pizza," he said.

Well, we didn't. But we gulped it down anyway, after extricating the pieces of pineapple from the melted cheese, hoping not too much juice had dripped from them. No such luck.

It didn't end there. The following night, the flight crew had the brilliant idea of stopping at a local

McDonald's and getting Quarter Pounders and fries for everybody on the plane. It wasn't the greatest, but when they threatened you with airplane food, they sort of had you over a barrel.

Again, we were looking forward to the hamburgers, if only for the change in menu. But, thanks to our boy Brian's dedication to the job, we showed up at the plane two hours late. Yes, the burgers were cold. We ate them anyway, trying not to taste them.

A cold McDonald's burger is quite a culinary experience. It tastes somewhat like a mushy hockey puck with ketchup. I christened it "Steak Trop-Tard."

So, you may understand that, the next night, when we ended up in a place called Wolseley, Saskatchewan, a hundred kilometres south of Regina, three of us decided to play hookie from the night's event and find a real restaurant to eat in, while Mulroney delivered his predictable speech.

A local advance woman told us we were in luck. Wolseley happened to be a sort of convention town south of the provincial capital, and had the best French restaurant in the province, called Le Parisien. Local boy Tim Naumetz couldn't believe it. "If there's a restaurant called Le Parisien in Wolseley," he said, "it's a story in itself!"

There was. And none of us could ever have suspected how "Parisian" it was. I found two accomplices to hit Le Parisien. As soon as we reached the campaign stop, Pierre April, from the Presse Canadienne, Hugues Poulin, from Radio-Canada and I dropped our gear inside the meeting room and made a bee-line for the restaurant, a few blocks away, in an old Victorian-style home.

Panting and heaving, we burst into the elegant restaurant, where we were greeted by a stunned hostess in an evening gown, standing under a crystal chandelier, with no intention of letting us through.

"We'd like to eat something quick," gasped my friend from radio.

"Do you have reservations?" she asked, dryly.

This was a time for Captain Gratton to come to the rescue. Drawing on my PMO experience, I played the power card. "We are travelling with the prime minister, and we're tired of eating sandwiches."

I'm not sure if she was shocked or impressed. Hesitantly, she said, "Maybe I can set you up a table in here." She pointed to a small table with a big flower pot on it, in the lobby.

To her astonishment we said "yes" whole-heartedly.

But she wasn't prepared for what was still in store. Hugues Poulin still had to file. Frantically, he asked for a telephone.

"If it's for a local call..." said the lady.

"That's fine, I've got a credit card," he answered, jumping on a telephone he had spotted right there in the lobby.

Right in the entrance of this fancy French restaurant, he got on his knees, whipped his tape recorder out of his bag and proceeded to take the receiver apart to plug in his alligator clips, while the hostess watched in horror.

April and I were looking at her with dumb smiles on our faces. She finally managed to stutter, "If what you need is a quick dinner, you can always go next door...they have pasta." We were gone as fast as we came, leaving our companion to tangle with her and her telephone. The fettucine sure was good.

Brian Mulroney himself ended up giving us our second great meal of the campaign, the following week, as we travelled to Saint John, New Brunswick. The prime minister was given a whole case of fresh lobster, as a gift from local union representatives.

That afternoon, we were served lobster in the press room. Mulroney had told media handler, Jacques Labrie, "Give this to the boys, but don't tell them it's from me."

But later on, after we had taken care of some of the best lobster I've ever eaten, he kept asking how the boys had liked it.

After two weeks with Mulroney, I sensed it was time to switch planes, when the silliness took over from the more sober campaign coverage. That was when we bums on the smoker's bus—nicknamed the Pizza Bus—started feuding with the straight crowd on the non-smokers bus—known as the Quiche Bus. (I don't smoke, but the Pizza bus had most of the fun people on it.)

It started with insults being exchanged over the buses' two-way radios, as we were travelling to the airport. Eventually, somebody in the Quiche bus said, "You know this means war!"

At that point, my buddy, Pierre April, stood up in his seat with a mean sparkle in his eyes and said, "Did they say war?"

We then started chanting wildly, "The Quiche Bus sucks!"

It didn't take us long to drown out the Perrier gang, as we carried our war chant onto the plane; so much so, that even some Quiche Bus passengers started chanting with us—agreeing with every word. It did suck.

I settled into my airplane seat for the flight home, and a ticket for the John Turner campaign. I was singing along to the songs The Doctor played on the ghetto blaster, from the Beatles to Randy Travis.

At the front of the plane, a curious Mulroney asked his executive assistant Rick Morgan, "Who's singing in the back?"

"Guess who?" said Morgan.

"No?"

"Yes."

# Chapter 8

On the first day, he sat on a giant pumpkin. On the second day, he paraded in a Ronald McDonald apron. On the third day, he gave a scrum standing in the mud.

Welcome to the John Turner campaign.

This was simply not the kind of politics I was used to. Sloppy, corny, unpredictable, just a little too human. Campaigns reflect candidates.

I hooked up with Turner's travelling circus in Vancouver. In fact, I had intended to link up with him in Edmonton, but my connecting plane from Ottawa to Toronto got stranded over the Pearson International Triangle. It circled the airport, waiting for a landing strip to clear for so long that I ended up in the never-never-land of air passengers who dare go through Toronto when they're in a hurry.

The fun part about that, of course, is getting your luggage back. Somehow, airlines find it hard to understand that you want your belongings off the plane.

"But it will follow you to Edmonton," says the smiling lady behind the counter.

"I'm not going to Edmonton anymore. I'm booked to Vancouver."

"Oh...well, then, we'll send it to Vancouver."

"You don't understand. We move from day to day. I'm covering the election campaign. You'll never catch up with me."

That's when you get that dirty, "are-you-putting-me-on?" look.

Finally, she relented and, with a heavy sigh, got some guy "on the ramp" at the other end of the phone. She didn't call me a jerk, but I'm sure something like that came to her mind. She finally told me to go wait at carousel number God-knows-what.

I followed her instructions, and ended up in a large waiting area of the biggest airport in Canada, all by myself. There was an absolutely immobile luggage carousel. At first, I expected somebody to show up but, after about fifteen minutes, I figured I was on my own. So I stared at that carousel intently, waiting for something to happen.

I don't know how much time went by. It seemed like an eternity. Then the noise came, and I almost fell on my back as the belt started to turn. And there it was, my flight-bag...but where was the other piece? The carousel stopped.

It's hard to describe the sinking feeling that came over me then, when I realized I had to go back to the friendly lady and explain to her that I actually had two pieces of luggage.

On that Tuesday, October 18, I was hopping on to a campaign that, according to the polls and everybody else who cared, was going nowehere. The only one to think otherwise was John Turner himself. As I got there, I marvelled at the man's resiliency under impending doom. How could he go on?

As it turned out, I happened to be covering John Turner for the two most important weeks of his campaign; the worst and the best.

As you can guess, the one that started with him sitting on a pumpkin was the worst. Having been trained on the "other side" with a stiff like Mulroney, I couldn't understand how a man who wanted to lead the country would sit on a giant fruit and smile that goofy smile, so that the world could see how hilarious he could be.

The next day was even weirder.

It was a typical rainy Vancouver morning. In the rain, when you can't see the mountains, that gorgeous city becomes very ordinary, almost depressing.

There we were at a McDonald's restaurant in Turner's riding of Quadra, for something called "McHappy Day," when the fast-food giant donated some of its receipts to charity.

John Turner was standing behind the counter, wearing a Ronald McDonald apron with "John Turner M.P." emblazoned across the front, just above the clown's face. This was the photo op to follow the one with the Great Pumpkin.

I suppose it wouldn't have been so bad, if only the candidate could have done what he was brought there to do: serve Big Macs and fries to the folks.

Except that, as he stood behind the counter,laughing his trademark staccato laugh and telling all the employees, many, many times, how "terrific" this all was, John Turner must have been wondering what the hell he was doing there. Because all he had in front of him was a wall of about fifty media spit-catchers, including seven TV camera crews. There were no customers, because whoever dared go through the door quickly retreated when confronted by the media obstacle.

Turner, meanwhile was left on his own by his inane staff. You can only say "it's terrific" so many times. To break the pattern, Turner turned to the employees in the kitchen and yelled, "How you doing back there?" Another staccato laugh. "It's terrific."

Finally, his hapless handlers managed to get a few customers through—most of them wearing Liberal buttons. After serving half a dozen burgers, Turner blurted out, "This is the most constructive thing I've done in the last three weeks!"

The boys on the bus were snickering. Another Turnerism for the books.

I felt strangely sad for the man. This was ridiculous. Mulroney's staff would never have led him into this kind of trap. Yet, somehow, John Turner genuinely seemed to be enjoying himself. Maybe I missed something.

That afternoon he gave a speech, followed by a question-and-answer session, at the University of British Columbia, his alma mater. About a thousand students showed up. I was shocked by the numbers. In a province where the Liberals hadn't elected anybody—except Turner—federally or provincially for years, he attracted so many young people. I was baffled.

He gave them what I described as his "TV evangelist number." He picked up the microphone in his right hand, put the other hand in his pocket and delivered his speech while walking back and forth across the stage. All the time, he was dragging his right leg, weakened by what was officially a "pinched nerve" in his back. (We learned later that it was actually caused by a benign tumorous growth near his spinal cord).

I was impressed. This man was possessed. It finally dawned on me in that university gymnasium. But the rest of the country, and Brian Mulroney, didn't know it yet.

And John Turner didn't suspect what thunderbolt would hit him that same night.

Nobody did. Except producer Elly Alboim and his top-notch CBC team in the national network's newsroom.

When it hit, it hurt. Peter Mansbridge, in that famous "trenchcoat report," revealed that a group of high-ranking Liberals, desperate to salvage the election, were ready to dump the leader in mid-campaign. The report was hastily staged, as Mansbridge did his stand-up outdoors on Wellington Street, while wearing a trenchcoat, to create the impression he was on assignment—something the CBC was ribbed about in the following weeks. The Liberals, at that point, were not just worried about losing; they were terrified that they would be obliterated from the Canadian political map, especially in Quebec.

Turner and his media herd were at Vancouver's Hyatt Regency Hotel. He was delivering a speech before a thousand supporters who had paid $250 a ticket for a fund-raising dinner—an astonishing number for any province in Canada, but truly unbelievable for Gritless B.C.

The news of the Mansbridge story spread like wildfire. Even the cynical media types found it hard to believe.

My friend Mike Duffy, who had just switched over to CTV, happened to be there for a special election report. He asked me what I thought.

"Guys like Elly and Peter don't risk their reputations on false stories," I said.

Duffy decided he was going to put me on the air for his Sunday show. He thought I was still close enough to the political world to offer at least an idea of how truly devastating such a story could be for Turner's team.

I was wearing a short-sleeved shirt with a huge duck and the inscription "King of Cool" on the front.

"Come on Duff, who's gonna take me seriously, dressed like this?"

"It'll be all right," he said, chuckling.

"Yeah, sure...I'm gonna tell the people how terrible this all is, and all the time they're gonna be staring at the duck on my shirt!"

After a few seconds of arguing, while his camera crew was hovering menacingly over me, he finally relented and let me pull my own Mansbridge coup. I agreed to do the interview, if he let me wear my trenchcoat. Except that, being indoors, it looked a little funny. The following week, I bumped into Duffy at the Ottawa Press Club, where he was discussing the interview with Don Newman, saying that it wrapped up his piece very well.

"Yes," said Newman," but you should have taken off your trenchcoat."

John Turner, meanwhile, had more serious problems. Nobody in the media listened to the speech he delivered to the sell-out crowd. The media wolves were just waiting for the wounded lamb to come limping by.

Turner didn't want to do it. His executive assistant, Doug Kirkpatrick, went up to him at the head table, explaining that he has no choice.

"Doug I don't want to do this!" insisted Turner, as his words were faintly caught by a TV boom mike. Squeezing his executive assistant's arm, he added, "If I do this, all it will be is a clip on TV...and all of this will be lost." This was a desperate, dejected man speaking, pleading with his employee to leave him alone.

Kirkpatrick didn't relent. He would have to face it sooner or later. Better to deny it all now and at least get his line out. Turner took a deep breath and grudgingly, dragging his bad leg, crossed the floor of the Hyatt Regency ballroom to meet with someone he already knew quite well: Disaster.

He said the only thing he could say: it was all nonsense. The spit-catchers had their clip, and ran to the phones.

I stayed behind. I couldn't help but feel for the man. Somehow, when politics is not numbers, TV images and slogans anymore, when an already-battered human being is standing there in front of you, being torn to pieces, the game pitting the media against THEM suddenly seems so unfair.

Maybe my three years on the dark side had softened me up, but I just couldn't see every politician as a bandit and a liar waiting to be exposed. Turner, in any case, was just too ordinary to fit the bill.

I was still milling about outside the ballroom when the event came to an end, and John Turner exited to go back to his lonely hotel suite. I just looked at him as he walked by. He saw me. I nodded hello. He gave me a look of deep despair and just shrugged, shaking his head. Somehow, he knew I understood. Or that, like him, I didn't.

The following day was a sombre one aboard the Turner plane. Even members of the media were at each other's throats, as arguments broke out about whether the CBC story made any sense or not. Turner's staff, of course, had every reason to fuel that disagreement. CBC reporter Keith Boag, on his first national campaign, got the brunt of the criticism, and could do nothing more than say he had nothing to do with it. But he was the closest thing to Peter Mansbridge they could find.

We flew all the way to Thunder Bay, Ontario, after an 8:00 a.m. Vancouver departure. There, the candidate visited a sawmill. I was used to them by now. It was about the fourth one I'd seen in three weeks of campaigning.

But this one had a special feature. It was muddy. With a drizzle, just bad enough to drive you up the wall, falling, Turner and the rest of us walked around in the mud for about an hour—or what seemed like an hour. Nobody was wearing rubbers. At the end of the tour, the Liberal leader gave a scrum, still wearing his hard hat.

This was getting more depressing by the minute.

My stomach was grumbling. It was late afternoon, and we hadn't eaten since breakfast. I asked Jane McDowell, one of Turner's press aides, "Is it because we've been bad that you're not feeding us?"

It was a joke but, under the circumstances, she took it as serious criticism.

It was time to go home. After a pit stop in Sault Ste. Marie, we eventually landed in Ottawa, at about 11:00 p.m. Everybody seemed relieved to jump off that cursed airplane.

There was one consolation. None of us was John Turner.

* * *

The phone rang early at my place, the next morning. I was officially up, but I wasn't too sure my body knew it.

As I picked up the receiver, the first word I heard was a resounding "Tabarnak!" That's French for just about every swear word you can imagine.

It was one of my Liberal friends, commenting on the events of the past few days and the plight of his leader. He wasn't concerned; he was terribly amused.

Then came the real shocker. "That's nothing," he said

of the CBC story. "You know that they asked Chretien to replace Turner, and he turned them down."

Now he had my attention.

"What did you just say?"

"I tell you, Chretien told them no way, because it's not his campaign, it's not his programme, they're not his candidates, they don't have any money..."

"Come on! Don't put me on. You mean they'd replace Turner with Chretien in mid-campaign?"

"Well, think about it. If they dump Turner, who will replace him?"

I was silent after that observation. It was so crazy it made sense. My informer then proceeded to give me details of who was involved in the coup, on the Quebec side of things. High on the list of conspirators were former Trudeau minister and Papineau MP Andre Ouellet and young Shefford MP Jean Lapierre, a former Turner backer who had changed camps the previous spring and tried to oust the leader.

I spent the whole day working on the story, along with my *Daily News* colleagues, Bernie St-Laurent and Peter Black. I managed to get Lapierre on his car phone. He denied any knowledge of such a plot, but he also sounded terrified on the telephone—not normal for Lapierre,who is always very self-assured. I was told later that, after he hung up with me, he was on the phone to another high-powered Liberal, to tell him that I had the goods on them.

With my colleagues checking their Montreal sources, we went with the story. But it had to be considerably watered down, since nobody wanted to go on the record. It was a frustrating story to write—and run—since we knew we were right, but we couldn't pin it down.

The next day, Jean Chretien denied it, but few members of the media believed him. And I was gratified, a year later, when Graham Fraser's excellent book on the election campaign, *Playing For Keeps*, basically confirmed that we had been right.

Yet, as all this was happening, I couldn't help but feel bad about digging John Turner's grave a little deeper.

Nobody, at that time, could have expected the turnaround that took place the following week. Other books and essays have been devoted to this, so I'll just say that John Turner came out of the two TV debates with flying colours, and soared to first place in the opinion polls.

It had its effect. Two days after the English debate, as Turner hit the campaign trail in Nova Scotia, there was free beer in the press room.

When I asked what the special occasion was, I was told that it had to do with the fact that we were in the Maritimes. I'm still trying to figure that one out.

But what I called "my gang" had just joined me from the Mulroney campaign—these were the rowdy reporters from the Pizza Bus, who had stayed on for one more week with the prime minister while I switched planes. I explained to them that the free beer was all an illusion; they barely fed us on this plane.

The fact was, though, that the Turner plane, in the end, enjoyed the most relaxed atmosphere of all three campaigns. Despite everything they'd been through—maybe because of it—they weren't as uptight as the Mulroney boys, and were allowed to have a drink once in a while.

It may have had something to do with the fact that the three most gorgeous women on any plane, from any carrier, from St. John's to Victoria, were keeping the media boys happy. Turner's two press aides, Catherine Cano and Jane McDowell, and his daughter Elizabeth were indeed a sight for the sore eyes of the males who had been away from home for too long.

In fact, Radio-Canada soundman Jean Labelle had a rather intriguing suggestion on the flight home from the Maritimes. Turner's handlers had organized what they called a "Beach Party." That's when everybody on the plane is expected to dress up as if...you got it, as if they're on a beach. Except they're in an airplane, see.

I hate organized fun, as a rule, and I found that idea especially childish, but I wasn't about to let that get in the way of myself and any fun to be had. Turner's slogan in the '88 campaign was "Let the people decide"—he was speaking, of course, of free trade.

But Jean Labelle had other ideas. He came up to me, to try and sell it, "I say, Elizabeth, Catherine and Jane all take off their clothes and let the people decide!"

It didn't happen. Not even close.

In fact, if there was one woman who enjoyed herself on that trip, it wasn't one of the three younger ones, it was Turner's wife, Geills. She merrily mixed with the media crowd, while wearing a foam boater that looked as though somebody had taken a big bite out of it. She got a kick out of taking pictures of everybody with her 35 mm camera.

The candidate himself drifted to the back of the plane and saluted, by blessing me with his right hand like a priest. He looked tired and strained. He surveyed the damage for a few seconds and smartly went back to his seat.

At that time, the Turner people were actually starting to believe they had a real chance of winning the election. At the very least, they weren't drowning, the way they had been for the first three weeks.

My view, however, was that there was too much time left—three weeks—and that Mulroney would turn it around. Because, other than his "Crusade for Canada" against free trade, Turner had nothing. His greatest weakness was that he had no team and, sooner or later, that would be exposed.

But, for one brief, beautiful moment, they were on top of the world. I wasn't going to rob them of that moment.

The time had come for me to do the toughest assignment of all: cover Ed Broadbent's campaign.

**Chapter** 9

Talk about boredom.

Switching planes to the NDP campaign is a lot like swallowing a bottle of Valium. The atmosphere is almost unreal. A feeling of total irrelevancy overtakes you as you contemplate the remote possibility of a socialist party—or is it socialistic, or even social democrat?—gaining power in middle-of-the-road Canada.

Oh, not every reporter feels that way. Some actually think they're on some kind of divine mission to give an equal chance to an underdog that has always cultivated its poor-working-man image, but gets most of its financing from big unions.

If this sounds like I don't have much time for the NDP, it's probably true. It's not their policies, it's not their political option, and it's not their members of parliament—most of whom are above average. It's the self-righteousness that gets to me. The holier-than-pure attitude about every cause they choose to defend.

Brian Mulroney doesn't like them very much, either. He used to say about Ed Broadbent that he had "the easiest job in the world," since he could stand up in the House of Commons, lambaste the government, call the prime minister a liar, be ejected by the speaker, and get away with it, all in the name of the people.

His wife, Mila, was a little more restrained on the matter. She realized that, in many cases, the NDP's political stands were extremely popular. On one of those days when Brian was doing his usual rant and rave about the leader of the New Democrats, she intervened to say, "Yeah...but he's on the right side of every issue."

Mulroney couldn't do anything but chew on his gum. Mila had a way of doing that to him like nobody else could.

\* \* \*

The first stop on the tour was Mississauga's City Hall, possibly the ultimate example of 1980s suburbia. The huge place looked like a set for a science fiction B-movie.

"Welcome to the planet Mars," said one of the media ruffians.

The most amazing thing was that it was practically deserted. There were not two hands to shake, and I wondered what on earth we were doing there. It was so empty, in fact, that I wondered if we were in the right place.

Ed Broadbent's brilliant strategists had brought him there to meet with the town's mayor, Hazel McCallion, a five-foot-tall no-nonsense pack of dynamite. She might have been in her sixties, but locally she was a legend you didn't mess around with. She was also not an NDP sympathizer. So, in fact, her meeting Broadbent was more a courteous public-relations exercise than a show of support.

For the leader of the NDP, though, it was a photo opportunity designed to "illustrate" the housing policy he would announce at noon. Mississauga, with its soaring house prices, was a good location to do that.

The mayor, however, seemed more interested in talking about her grandiose Council Chambers, and how the

Duke and Duchess of York were "very impressed by them." Didn't sound like socialist talk. The Council Chambers in question were, in fact, something to see. They were somewhat like a Roman forum in royal blue and white, with pictures that looked like the zodiac signs painted on the ceiling, some thirty feet above the floor.

This was not only insignificant, it was weird. I was lonesome already.

Broadbent followed that impressive number up with a glad-handing session in a shopping centre that was, understandably, also half-empty in the middle of a working day. I didn't pay much attention to what went on, as the usual media pack, with their phalanx of cameras and microphones, dutifully followed in the steps of the NDP leader.

At one point, I was fascinated by an aquarium display of what looked like piranhas, in the window of a pet store. As I was totally absorbed in my observations, I looked up, to see that Ed Broadbent was only a few feet away and looking straight at me.

I nodded to say "hello," since we'd known each other professionally for some time.

He pointed to the aquarium, and said to me, "The Tory caucus..."

I smiled, assuming he was referring to the fact that my demise as a press secretary started with comments made about myself—and my cohort, Bill Fox—in Mulroney's national caucus, which ate us alive, like a school of piranhas.

It had been a long time since I'd even nodded at Broadbent. As I wrote in my previous book, I had not forgiven him yet for the fact that he let a member of his caucus—Margaret Mitchell—attack me in the House of Commons, over rather vague accusations of my asking women from the Press Gallery out for dates.

In fact, after leaving the PMO, when I attended the annual Press Gallery dinner, I confided in his wife, Lucille—whom I have a lot of admiration for—that, "I'm still mad at your husband." I've often wondered if she ever gave him the message.

I was stunned, however, after our visit to Mississauga, when I got back on the bus, to bump into one of Broadbent's key aides, a woman I hardly knew, who told me point-blank, "I want you to know that I never agreed with them raising that in the House."

I was dumbfounded. I just didn't know what to say. After all this time, people still had my sad adventure on their minds. And, although she couldn't change the past, she still made me feel good, whoever she was.

But, back to the campaign trail. A few hours later, after Broadbent had explained a complex housing strategy that few people understood and fewer cared about, we hopped on the plane.

Thank God my Press Club pal, *Sun* columnist Joe O'Donnell, was also condemned to the Broadbent campaign for the week. At least I'd have comic relief and a drinking buddy.

He suggested, brilliantly, that we take a seat at the back of the plane, "away from the dorks." He also pointed out convincingly that we would get preferred service in the last seat of the DC-9.

I don't know why I believed him, but I did. As it turned out, we got the worst service on the aircraft, and we ended up right in the middle of Dork City.

During the first month of the campaign, somebody had the bright idea of installing a miniature basketball net on the wall at the back of the plane. It came with a little foam ball, and was designed for children to play with. I guess it was perfect for the media. As a result, though, O'Donnell and I ended up sitting in the middle of a basketball court, while the boys amused themselves and we couldn't get served. Great.

I was quickly sinking into deep depression.

The fact that we were landing in exciting downtown Thunder Bay that night did nothing to lift my spirits.

The next morning, the wake-up call came at dawn. It was a funny kind of dawn, in the fall in Northern Ontario, at 6:00 a.m.. Maybe because it was still pitch dark.

It was also -4C, and you could see a thin coat of ice

shining like a mirror in the moonlight, on the streets of the city on the shores of Lake Superior. Freshly out of bed, at an hour when I usually have just crawled into it, I was shivering. *God, what am I doing here? Mulroney and Turner don't do this kind of stuff!*

No. This was a typical NDP campaign tactic—although local candidates from all parties have adopted it, leaders other than Broadbent rarely do it. It has been dubbed "plant-gating." That's when the candidate stands at the entrance to a factory or a mill, to greet Joe Lunchbox as he goes in to work in the morning.

I'm not sure how effective it is, but these are the people the NDP believes to be their natural constituency, the workers. I happen to believe, myself, that a lot of the people who vote for them are already-well-off yuppies who can afford to vote socialist. But I suppose the statistics wouldn't entirely back my theory.

In any case, Broadbent either believed, or had been convinced, that this was a good idea; otherwise no leader in his right mind would have submitted himself to it.

All of a sudden, the media pack became animated. They had found a worker, a scraggly-haired youngster who said he was going to vote for Brian Mulroney because he believed in free trade.

It didn't take long for an older worker to intervene in the discussions, while the cameras were rolling, and to set the kid straight. Charles Meeking recited a litany of statistics to justify his opposition to Mulroney and free trade. This guy knew his stuff better than Broadbent, for crissake!

As I learned later, he should. He was the president of the Thunder Bay Labour Council and the NDP's union contact for this campaign event—although he didn't boast about it too loudly before the media.

After trying to shut the kid up, all the time calling him "Brother," he finally pulled him away from the media and led him inside the plant. All the way, of course, he was pursuing his attempt at indoctrination.

When a reporter finally asked him who he was to have the authority to drag the other worker inside, he simply explained that he was "the plant inspector." Yeah, right. And a union leader, and an NDP organizer.

Democracy and freedom of speech the socialist way, I guess. When things don't go right, pull them out of the limelight.

When the event was finally over, Charles Meeking shook Broadbent's hand vigorously. Ed said "Thank you."

I wrote a column about the whole thing for the next day's *Daily News*.

On the Tory campaign plane, as one of his aides confided to me later, Mulroney "is having an orgasm," reading about the incident in my column.

"Look at this! Read this! See, that Broadbent!" he said.

Of course I was totally unsuspecting of the reaction my prose was provoking thousands of miles away. All I could think about was that I was a prisoner in this torture chamber for another two weeks, knowing Broadbent would finish third.

Ed knew it too by now, although he didn't always believe that. At the beginning of the campaign, when the polls were showing the Tories in first place and the NDP second, with Turner's Liberals lagging far behind, Broadbent was boasting that the people of Canada had finally understood that the real choice was between a party on the right and one on the left. The wishy-washy Grits were bound to disappear, as had happened in other countries like Great Britain.

At the time, Mulroney, asked about Broadbent's comments, had been careful to say that he thought the Liberals were a lot more resilient than that. Now, with three weeks to go, the Liberals were first, the Tories second, and the NDP had fallen to its traditional third spot. While I listened in amazement, Broadbent explained how this meant that the Tories were finished, and so was free trade.

I wrote in *The Daily News* that he'd better be careful. If he kept up his dire predictions, Mulroney would end up winning the election. That was the only prophecy he hadn't made yet.

When we finally got back on the plane to leave Thunder Bay behind, our next destination was to be another northern jewel, Kenora.

Now, I don't remember much about the Kenora event itself, but I still have nightmares about the fancy landing our damned DC-9 made on the one and only runway of Kenora's international airport.

I knew we were in trouble when the pilot announced there was a strong crosswind, and the aircraft started circling like a bird of prey. I had flown often enough to know what that meant.

"I hate these landings," I told my companion, O'Donnell, as I suspected what was coming next.

The plane then dipped to the left and kept on circling, while all the time losing altitude. This produced a rather strange effect. On one side of the aircraft, the passengers could only see the ground below—that was my situation. On the other side, they could only see the sky, since the plane was virtually flying with its wings at a vertical angle.

We circled and circled and circled, while I turned progressively whiter, and a deadly silence fell on the cabin. The ground got closer and closer, until it seemed the tip of the wing could almost touch it. The pilot then pulled down the plane to the other side and we landed, with all the grace of a manhole cover running on its rim.

"We landed on two wheels!" I gasped in disbelief.

"No, that can't be," said O'Donnell.

"I tell you, we did! We landed on the front wheel and the wheel under our wing..."

Still shaken up, I was determined to clear the whole thing up with the commander of the aircraft. As I was the last one off—being seated in the last row—I happened to see him inspecting the outside of the plane as I got off.

"Do you mind if I ask you something?" I said. "Did we land on two wheels?"

"Yes, we did," he answered, matter-of-factly.

"Do you mind telling me why?"

He went on to explain how, with a strong crosswind

and only one runway to choose from, this was a perfectly normal manoeuvre.

"If you don't compensate, the wind could blow you off the runway," he explained.

"Oh," I said. I went to turn back, then, as an afterthought, I asked him, "Is that easy to do?"

"No, not really," he said, simply.

"Oh...How about when we take off. Is it just as difficult?"

"Well," he answered, "it's a little harder to miss the sky."

And he didn't. Which explains how we landed in Regina a few hours later.

We were scheduled to bus south to Moose Jaw that evening, and come back to the hotel in Regina later that night. I missed the bus, after dozing off in my room. I'm not used to six o'clock wake-up calls.

As I awoke suddenly and looked at the bedside clock, I realized I would never get to see Moose Jaw.

I phoned the desk in Montreal, more to cover my ass than to apologize.

Jim Duff, my managing editor, came on the line.

"What's up?" he asked.

"I just missed the bus to Moose Jaw."

"Moose Jaw! Oh gawd, man, bail out of there! Get on the next plane to Ottawa. That campaign is irrelevant."

"You don't have to tell me twice."

I got back on the phone to Ottawa and to my girlfriend (now my wife), Christine, and said, "Baby, I'm coming home!" I hadn't been that happy in a long time.

That night, when I saw my friend O'Donnell in the hotel restaurant, I told him, beaming, "I'm leaving the campaign."

"Oh, man," he said, "you're not leaving me here alone?"

But I did. My two weeks with Ed Broadbent turned into a three-day affair.

What can I say? I was restless to see my old friend Brian again.

# Chapter 10

**N**ow, that was more like it.

The movie *Trains, Planes and Automobiles*, starring John Candy and Steve Martin, was playing on the TV. I was enjoying every hilarious minute of it.

Those Tories really knew how to put on a show. Because, you see, the hit movie was being shown on Brian Mulroney's campaign aircraft, the Boeing 727 that his team has christened "The Baie Comeau Express," but that the media had re-named "No-Comment-Air." (That, of course, had nothing to do with the fact that the prime minister had been carefully avoiding the press, except for staged "spontaneous" scrums, since the beginning of the campaign.)

How on earth did they manage to get a TV and a VCR on board—and make them work? As a matter of fact, they had a couple of sets going, to help pass the time away on the five-hour flight from Ottawa to Vancouver. All part of the wizardry of a Tory team, with seemingly unlimited financial and human resources, that was doing everything to please, at this stage of the campaign.

What a difference a month makes.

The last time I had sat there was at the end of the second week of this seven-week bout. Everything was coming up roses for the Tories and their champion, whose biggest concern was not to appear too over-confident in public. I learned later that the Tory strategists were already concerned about a certain "slippage" in the polls, in favour of the Liberals, even before John Turner's triumphant performance in the TV debates. But it certainly wasn't showing in their public behaviour.

The Mulroney team simply appeared unconcerned, and eager to end the massacre.

The Boss himself was rather bored with what he was being asked to do—the Tory strategy calling for him to keep a very low-profile, so-called "prime ministerial" tone. In fact, Mulroney prided himself on being one of the best on-the-stump campaigners in the country, and he was probably right. To run a campaign where he let his opponents take daily pot-shots, without returning the fire, was sheer torture to him.

So, in the early days of the 1988 campaign, he was feeling rather miserable in his protective bubble, and would often complain aloud to his entourage, "They want me to shut up, I shut up!"

That meant, of course, that he thought the whole thing was utterly ridiculous, and that he would be far more effective doing what he did best; swinging back, instead of dancing away from the blows.

Now things had changed, following Turner's stunning debate victory.

The Tories were pulling out all the stops to try and reverse the anti-free-trade trend that Turner appeared to have successfully generated. They were trotting out just about anybody who would say something positive about free trade, and something bad about the Grits, before the cameras. From Robert Bourassa to Simon Reisman, to the father of medicare, ninety-year-old Emmett Hall, they were all doing their bit to save Brian Mulroney from humiliation. Big Business jumped into the fray, with cross-country ads that later brought the wrath of Elections Canada chairman Jean-Marc Hamel, but couldn't legally be stopped. By the end of the contest, Mulroney even had his buddies, Ronald Reagan and Margaret Thatcher, plead his free trade case for him. Chances were, Canadians had more confidence in them than in him.

So in this, the last week of the campaign, the Tory team was going into the home stretch with their tongues hanging out, their jockeys whipping like crazy, and their minds fixed on a photo finish they wished had never happened.

As for Mulroney himself, he was now talking in ways his strategists had found undesirable, earlier in the contest. He was giving a more visionary speech and, at long last, he was throwing the insults back at his adversaries.

What was he calling them? Well, liars, of course. Everybody was a liar in this campaign, if you listened to the speeches of all three leaders. Mulroney was finally in his element. He would win the campaign himself—or at least that's what he believed. He also knew that he had to make up for his poor performance in the TV debates, not only for the electorate but, strangely, for the people surrounding him. A Godfather does not like to be humbled in front of his capos.

So he was going all out, damn the torpedoes.

And then there was the flag.

It finally dawned on me in Calgary, the next day. This was not any flag—it was THE FLAG, the Canadian red maple leaf in living colour. Brian Mulroney had just discovered it, maybe because he noticed John Turner had been wearing it like a mantle, since he had started his "Crusade for Canada."

The Boss decided he was going to be the most Canadian of all the Canadians who wanted to be prime minister. But he needed a backdrop, so his boys found him a twenty-by-forty-foot zinger of a flag.

It looked so impressive that an American reporter gasped, "I've never seen a flag that big! Even at a George Bush rally!"

Well, not to out-Yank the Yanks, but the Tories actually had another, even bigger, forty-by-eighty-foot one stashed somewhere, in case their leader's patriotism is challenged further.

Mulroney was pumped up, in front of a two-thousand-strong, cheering crowd, at a noon rally in this traditional Tory stronghold.  There were hecklers there, but he played off them effectively.  He told them they didn't have to worry about being "carried out on a stretcher," if they voiced their opinions at a Conservative rally.

He was referring to an ugly incident that took place several miles away in Pierrefonds, Quebec, where Liberal supporters beat up a Tory heckler.  The picture of the bloodied young man ran in every newspaper in the country and Mulroney, who knew gutter politics, was milking it for all it was worth.

At first, he told the hecklers not to worry, they wouldn't be "assaulted" at one of his rallies; then he said they didn't need their first-aid kits to come here; by the time he finished, hyperbole on cue, he pulled out the "stretcher" line.

Amazing what a little blood can do to boost a campaign. Vintage Mulroney.

He was going after Turner, calling him "John The Ripper." Any connection with "Jack The Ripper?" Nah...mere coincidence. Mulroney was using the expression to ridicule Turner's contention that he would "tear up" the free trade agreement, once elected.

It sounded corny.  But in the political era of the two-minute TV clip, corny works.

And this was the real Mulroney.  The prime-ministerial style that he sometimes strangely craved, simply didn't suit him.

As my American colleague pointed out, "All pitchers want to be hitters...and all street-fighting politicians want to be statesmen."

But Brian is stuck with his street-fighting self.  And he's not a man who likes to be pushed around.

One demonstrator learned the hard way, during the 1988 campaign.  Throughout the seven-week struggle,

Mulroney was often confronted by demonstrators, mostly anti-free-trade, some anti-nuclear-submarines, and some just plain angry. The latter were the ones he simply couldn't stand.

As he had told me many times before, he knew that his second election would be rougher than the first, in 1984, when demonstrators started to appear only in the final days of the struggle, as it became certain he was going to be elected prime minister.

"You know, Michel," he would say, when we were confronted by a demo, "during the next campaign we're going to get this everywhere we go...better get used to it."

The prediction had certainly come true in 1988.

But, biding his time and biting his lip on his campaign bus, he was promising himself a little treat every time he peered out of the window to see that he was going to be greeted by a savage crowd one more time.

Mila kept trying to hold him back, but she knew that, sooner or later, he was going to do it. And it happened, as the story was told to me, in Peterborough. Mulroney walked through a crowd of angry demonstrators. He walked over to the biggest screaming man he could find, and signalled him, with his index finger, to bend over.

When the puzzled man did, the prime minister said in his ear, "Fuck you, asshole!"

That sort of shut him up.

Smiling and waving to the crowd, Mulroney got back on his bus, with Mila screaming about how unreasonable he was. The smile never left his face.

The story didn't surprise me. He had done roughly the same thing, four years earlier, on the last day of the campaign, in the rough Labrador iron-ore town of Wabush.

He had been met there by a really angry crowd of demonstrators, who went as far as rocking his bus when he left the meeting hall.

Just before he hopped on the bus, he said in the ear of one of the angry men, in French, "Eat shit, mon tabarnak."

The last part is a French swear word that cannot be

translated, but it's roughly the equivalent of "asshole."

Once in a while, the prime minister also likes to prove how smart he is.

Take two days after the Calgary meeting, in Montreal, for instance.

It was just another rally at some local candidate's headquarters. This one was taking place in Claude Lanthier's riding of LaSalle-Emard, where the Liberal opponent was none other than Paul Martin, Jr., who would win and later run for the party leadership.

Mulroney was sitting on his private bus with his key aides, a couple of hours before it began. He was working on a speech, scribbling notes on a piece of paper, as he often does. His masterpiece completed, he called his press secretary, Marc Lortie, over.

"Okay, Marc, what do you think?" he asked, testing some nasty line he wanted to say about John Turner.

Whatever it was, Lortie told him he thought it was a little too strong.

Then Mulroney gave him another line, where he called the opponents of free trade "the Luddites" of the election campaign.

A blank look came over Lortie's face.

"What's a Luddite?" asked the former diplomat, who is rarely at a loss on matters of that kind.

Feigning indignation, Mulroney said, "You don't know what a Luddite is?"

He went on to explain happily that the obscure expression referred to those who were opposed to the industrial revolution in England, two centuries ago. A Luddite, therefore, is somebody who stands in the way of inevitable progress—like the opponents of free trade, of course.

"I don't think people will understand what you're talking about," said Lortie.

Mulroney pondered the advice for a few seconds and said, "Okay...I'll drop the thing about Turner, but I'm keeping the Luddites!"

And he did.

I was standing at the back of the room, on the riser

provided for the TV cameras. All of a sudden, he dropped the bomb. A young TV soundman standing next to me instinctively put his hands on his earphones, thinking something must be wrong with his equipment.

Then Mulroney said it again.

With a baffled look on his face, the poor guy took one earphone off and asked me, "What's a Luddite?"

I was just as stumped as he was. And so were the few hundred Tory supporters in the room, and most of the other members of the media corps.

In fact, a lot of us thought he had mis-spoken, and meant to say something else, especially to a francophone audience like this one.

After finding out that he actually had said exactly what he wanted to say, and what Luddites were, I got a lot of humorous mileage out of it.

When we got back on the bus, I asked one of Mulroney's media handlers, the one we called Boomer, "Hey, what's a Luddite?"

He answered, "You want a low-diet what?"

But you have to hand it to Mulroney. His "Luddite" quote went around the country. The treatment *The Globe And Mail* gave it the next day was particularly funny, since it seemed like half the front-page story was taken up explaining who the Luddites were.

I told you. Corny works.

If only because we weren't able to take too many more bad lines, it was time for this campaign to come to an end. And it was with a great sense of relief that we boarded No-Comment-Air, to make the trip to our final destination before the big vote: Baie Comeau, where else?

The press rowdies like Baie Comeau. First of all, it's not too big, so anywhere you have to go is not far. And, whenever he goes there, Mulroney doesn't do very much and is usually in a good, easy-going mood.

But the most well-kept secret of the media's attraction to Baie Comeau is Madame Lecompte. She's the owner and operator of the motel that bears her name, and she treats the members of the national media better than she would her own kids—especially during an election campaign.

This time around, for instance, she provided two back-to-back all-night parties on the last weekend of the campaign, after the regular bar and restaurant had closed. She had done the same thing four years earlier, and the boys who had been there at the time remembered it.

The motel itself was no big deal, if you excluded the so-called "nuptial suite," with its round bed, shag carpeting and comforter to match and, of course, mirrors. Every time we ended up there, the big question was who had the "nuptial suite."

That was, in fact, rather tame, compared to the Caravelle motel across the highway, which offered an exclusively-pornographic channel on the tube. Everybody had seen it, but few journalists would admit to it.

But the Lecompte was sort of a home away from home. When I was in the PMO, I had the choice of staying at the motel or the plush Manoir Comeau, an old stone building that was considered to be the town's answer to the Ritz-Carlton.

When he travels to his home town, Mulroney stays in a huge guest cottage located next to the Manoir, a few hundred feet from the house he was born in.

But I wasn't crazy about the Manoir, because I didn't find there the typical Quebec warmth and openness that Madame Lecompte gave us. So, I would tell the prime minister that I had "to be with the boys," and would book myself at the motel as often as I could.

Another one of our favourite hang-outs in town was the Verdi restaurant, which served everything from Italian to seafood. We would take great pride in emptying their wine cellar.

All this is to say that, whenever we hit Baie-Comeau, the temperature of the whole campaign seemed to go down. Life appeared a little easier and slower.

We also knew the end was finally near.

It was a mellow Monday, November 21. Three separate opinion polls had just indicated, two days earlier, that

Mulroney had succeeded in totally reversing the numbers with Turner, and that he could now claim anywhere between forty-one and forty-three per cent of the vote, with the Grits somewhere between thirty-two and thirty-five.

As I had suspected all along, it seemed that Mulroney would salvage a majority, thanks principally to his strength in Quebec. He would owe a big one to Robert Bourassa, once elected. Quebec had been at the centre of his strategy all along. He believed that, if he could get as many as, if not more than, the fifty-eight (out of seventy-five) seats he had gotten in the province in 1984, he would win enough elsewhere—especially in the Conservative West—to preserve his majority. Ideally, he thought that, if Ontario voters sensed that Quebec was going massively his way, they also would topple on his side, so as not to be left in the Liberal dark.

In the end, our homegrown version of Machiavelli was right.

I was sitting in the press room, set up for the occasion at the Baie Comeau arena, when the results started coming in. Again, I had a sense of *deja vu* as I remembered that, four years earlier, I was also sitting there, anticipating a major victory. I was a little more detached this time but, in a strange way I couldn't quite understand, I felt I was still part of the Mulroney team—maybe because I could feel for so many of my true friends still on the other side of the fence.

One of them, Jacques Labrie, was sitting next to me. He had been a friend for a long time, before my days with Mulroney, when he was a TV producer and I a columnist at *Le Droit*. But I was the one who had brought him into this Tory mess, and I couldn't help but secretly cheer for him—and others like him.

As the results from the Maritimes started to come in, shortly after 8:00 p.m., a frown came over Labrie's face. They were down 20-12.

"We were expecting to win at least two more there," he said, simply.

He didn't worry for very long. At 8:37 p.m., the CBC

announced that Brian Mulroney had repeated a feat unequalled since Louis Saint-Laurent had done it in 1953, winning two majorities in a row.

He was down to 169 seats, from 211, but that was enough. The Liberals had 83, and the NDP, 43.

Brian Mulroney was alone in a room on the second floor of the Manoir Comeau, as the results came in. Mila, the kids and a handful of close aides were downstairs, knowing he wanted to be left alone.

It was quite different from four years earlier, when Mulroney had many of his friends and cronies gathered around him for what everybody expected to be a celebration. A sign of power and the times.

When the CBC predicted the big win, a cheer went up from the few people in the cottage, and members of the family and staff all rushed upstairs.

A beaming Mulroney greeted them with, "Sir John A. would be proud of his pony tonight."

He had done the impossible. Faced with a reluctant electorate, weighed down by scandals and a shaky first mandate, he had survived, as even Pierre Elliott Trudeau couldn't. At long last, he had shaken the monkey off his back. At long last, he was really prime minister.

That night, Brian Mulroney went over to the main building of the Manoir Comeau, where staffers and friends were assembled to celebrate the victory, and belted out a few of his favourite tunes. He was a very happy man.

Meanwhile, the members of the media, once the last results were in somewhere past midnight, took over the Lecompte for a celebration of their own. Somewhere around 3:00 a.m., they were joined by the PMO staffers, who had been models of restraint for the previous seven weeks. For one brief night, the "fence" didn't exist anymore, and nobody cared what the others did.

I missed it. I had collapsed in my bed around two o'clock. Age, you know.

The next day, the re-elected prime minister was all smiles at his press conference.

As they did regularly, the boys had tried to pump me

up before the press conference. They wanted me to ask my first question to Mulroney as a reporter.

"The man won't even look at me," I said. "If you think I want to make a fool of myself..."

Mulroney, who hadn't acknowledged my existence for over a year, even when I was standing only a few feet away, had, nevertheless, come very close to speaking to me earlier in the campaign.

It was a totally unexpected situation, both for him and for me.

We were in Yarmouth, Nova Scotia. I had deliberately slept in and missed the early-morning event. We were scheduled to leave right after it, however, so I headed straight for the airport in a cab as soon as I was ready to go.

When I got to the aircraft, nobody was back yet. The air crew was there, though, so I got on the plane and sat down in my seat, reading a magazine, with the whole place to myself.

A few moments later, I heard people come in through the back door of the plane. I expected to see some of my media buddies arrive, since the prime minister always came in through the front door.

Out of the blue, I heard a female voice say, "Bonjour, Michel."

I thought I recognized the voice, but I couldn't believe it. I looked up to see Mila Mulroney walking up the aisle.

"Bonjour Madame," I answered simply.

Then I could feel the "other" presence, as he passed my seat. I suddenly grew very tense. Was this going to be it?

Brian Mulroney walked slowly by, with his hands in his pant pockets. He had heard his wife speak to me, I knew. I braced myself for the worst. From the corner of the eye that I was trying to keep on the magazine, I saw him hesitate for a fraction of a second. But no. He wasn't ready yet. The doghouse was still mine.

So, on the morning after the election, although I knew the man was in a super mood, there was still no way I was going to expose myself to his wrath publicly.

However, I might have had a modest part in the press conference, anyway. Before it started, some of the boys were asking themselves what would be a good question. I happened to mention that, back in 1983, when he had been chosen as leader of the party, Mulroney had told a group of Quebec reporters (of which I was one), in an off-the-record conversation, that he didn't believe a prime minister should stay for more than two four- or five-year terms.

Well, as we sat there waiting to gobble up Brian's words of wisdom, Southam reporter Les Wittington got up, and guess what he asked. Right. "Do you intend this one to be your last term, as you said back then?"

That time, an amused Mulroney, with a sarcastic grin on his face, looked straight at me, sitting about twenty feet in front of him. He tilted his head sideways toward the reporter, in a sign that meant, "Can you believe this guy?"

That was almost as good as talking to me. I sensed, at that moment, that my rehabilitation was under way.

Wittington said, "I don't want to get rid of you, but..."

Mulroney interrupted quickly. "You've been giving it your best shot...give me a break, Mr. Wittington."

He also said, later, "Someone said, 'Let the people decide.' The people have decided."

Four more years.

# Chapter 11

If there's one thing that has constantly fascinated me about Brian Mulroney, both when I worked for him and after I left, it's how much the man tries to hide his past.

It's as if anything he did before being elected leader of the Conservative party, in 1983, never happened. He wants people to know him for what he does as a politician, and is paranoid about things that may shed a different light on the kind of person he was back when...

I never quite understood why. It is true that we are all voyeurs, and that Ottawa has become our poor man's Hollywood, for lack of another star community. It's also true that we all have skeletons in our closets that we would not necessarily want the world to know about. And, of course, when one is prime minister of the country, certain revelations can be rather embarrassing.

But I've always thought, personally, that Mulroney's obsession with keeping his past a secret only had the opposite effect: the more he tried to hide it, the more people sought to find it out. As a result, some pretty wild stories have come up about the era of Brian's life known as his "carousing days."

The expression, of course, refers to his now-extinct penchant for alcohol and beautiful women. He can fudge a lot of things, but Brian Mulroney can never deny that, in his free-wheeling bachelor days, which lasted until age thirty-five, he enjoyed a lot of both.

Coming from me, that is far from an accusation.

The following anecdote might indicate how we both feel about it.

It was toward the end of the 1984 campaign. We were in Montreal, staying, as usual, at the chic Ritz-Carlton. I was then deputy press secretary to Bill Fox.

Nights in Montreal can make a grown man humble. It felt like I had just gone to bed, and I needed a lot more sleep when the phone rang in my room at 7:00 a.m.. Fox was on the line.

"I've set up a breakfast interview with The Boss for Pierre April (from the Press Canadienne). Can you go?"

"Jesus, I just crawled into bed," I mumbled.

"Well, all you have to do is stagger about fifty feet!" Fox answered.

I couldn't argue with that kind of logic. The interview was scheduled to start in about ten minutes.

Painfully, I dragged myself out of bed, put on the same wrinkled clothes I'd worn the night before, and walked down the hall to the room where April was already waiting for me. Being a buddy of mine, he wasn't surprised to see me in such damaged condition.

Then Mulroney walked in. He took one look at me and said, with a wicked smile, "You were out last night, Michel?"

He then quickly turned to April, and added, "It's not a reproach, it's envy."

But, apart from occasional cracks like that one, Mulroney was very discreet about even alluding to his crazier past with people like me, who were not longtime friends. As a matter of fact, his so-called cronies were equally discreet about it. They knew he didn't want anybody to talk about it.

I learned about the fear of God he inspired in people he had known during those forgotten days, very early in the mandate. The following story is a perfect example of what happens when somebody talks too much about the Godfather.

It was back in early 1985. I was doing some advance work for the famous visit of Ronald Reagan to Quebec City, on March 17 and 18, the Shamrock Summit.

We were desperately looking for a St. Patrick's event in which the two Irish leaders could participate.

Quebec CBC reporter Bernie St-Laurent, who knew the town like the back of his hand, told me, "You have to go to Noonan's Pub! You can't do something on St. Pat's day in Quebec City without going to Noonan's Pub!"

In fact, the bar, called Le Chien d'or, had been one of Brian Mulroney's favourite hang-outs, during his Laval University days. But it was then located within the Old Town of Quebec, near that famed landmark, the Chateau Frontenac.

It had been moved out to the suburb of Ste-Foy in recent years, and was now called simply "Le Pub"—a sure sign of the decline of the once-thriving Irish community in that historic French city.

I went over to scout the place with PMO advance man Marc Allard. Marc was a happy-go-lucky, rotund man, who liked to laugh and was totally dedicated to his job. He reminded me, in his manner and his way of approaching people, of a travelling salesman eager to please. He was so committed to the job that, during the 1984 campaign, he was on the road so much he had to buy big flushable diapers, because he was out of clean underwear.

We were met at a pub that was quite empty in the middle of the afternoon. It was a nice modern brasserie, in the usual Quebec mode. The owner, Mr. Noonan, was mighty happy to see us, when we told him why we were there.

We sat down to have a few draughts with him and discuss the possibility of having the President of the

United States and the Prime Minister of Canada make him famous.

I mentioned something about the fact that Mulroney himself apparently used to be a regular at the pub, when it was located in the *Vieille Ville*. I could see that Noonan appeared a little uneasy about it.

He explained that he knew "a lot of stories" about Mulroney and his antics in those days.

"But one day," he said to Allard and me, "I told some of those stories. The message came back from Brian—through somebody else—that stories should stay where and when they happened."

*The Godfather had spoken*, I thought.

I was burning to ask him to tell a few, and swear I'd never say where I got them, but I couldn't pressure the poor soul. As it turned out, he never got to see the PM and the president, since Brian opted, instead, to sing a verse of "When Irish Eyes Are Smiling" on the stage of Quebec's Grand Theatre.

But this apparently insignificant incident showed me, not only how important it was to The Boss to forget his past, but to what lengths he was ready to go to get his way.

So, for all the times I was alone with Mulroney when we really didn't have much to talk about, I was very careful not to appear to pry too much into his former life. But there were moments when the subject came up.

It almost always happened on the Challenger jet, at the end of a long day, when the prime minister would let himself go.

There have been a lot of stories and rumours about Brian Mulroney's reasons for quitting drinking. Some of them have been pretty unfair, as such stories often are, I suppose. The worse it is, the better.

Well, all I can give you is the explanation from the horse's mouth, which came unexpectedly on one of those flights back home.

As I remember it, I think I was drinking a glass of wine, as we sometimes did on the plane, when the day and the week were over. (Somehow I doubt they even do that now.)

The Boss made an inoffensive comment about it, and I blurted out, "Do you ever miss it?"

I guess, at the time, I was thinking more of my own case, knowing I would find it extremely hard to quit drinking entirely.

He shook his head. "No...not at all. You know, Michel, even when I was drinking, I never drank at noon and I never missed a day's work," he said.

Thinking back on the conversation now, I'm not sure whether he was saying that for himself, or as a message to me. Mulroney still has a way of disguising his messages like that. It's almost like a bible parable. You have to guess at it and, in Mulroney's entourage, few people do right away.

He went on to explain how he quit. "I was having dinner with Jean Bazin (the close friend he appointed to the Senate) one day, about a month before Christmas. I said to Jean, 'Say, why don't we skip the wine today?' I decided to quit drinking until Christmas...I never had another drink."

All I've ever seen him drink is soda water and coffee. Lots of it. Sometimes both at the same time, a habit that somehow puzzled me.

So that's his side of the story. I thought I'd tell it, since it's highly unlikely he will ever do so himself.

He doesn't seem to mind being around people who drink or are drunk, as he demonstrated several times, by staying awake with the media rowdies at the National Press Club half the night, singing songs at the piano with people who could hardly talk.

But he did comment once on the fact that some people really became miserable when they stopped drinking. He gave a few examples of such cases, as if he just couldn't understand it.

He also commented once in Montreal, after a luncheon, that businessmen's noon drinking habits sure had changed. "Look at that," he said in the limousine. "It used to be double martinis. Now they're drinking spritzers."

It was just an observation about how society was changing on the matter that he had settled for himself some time before.

In a strange—but perhaps very perceptive—way, he seemed to link alcohol and womanizing. And he obviously thought I had both diseases.

He often imagined that I had some kind of devious plan in my head to pick up women while we were on assignment. He wasn't always wrong, but he gave me far too much credit since, for most of the time I spent working for him, I went out with two different women—and it was serious. Of course, I also had my bad moments, which were well documented in the press.

I remember one occasion, when we were in Baie Comeau. My girlfriend, Ann Charron, who worked in my office, had to stay behind, while I normally should have hopped on the plane back to Ottawa that same night with the PM.

In the course of the day, I happened to phone Bill Fox, back in the capital.

"I'd really like to stay here, and come back tomorrow with the technicians," I said. "Ann's here, and I haven't seen her in a few days." I was really musing, more than asking for permission.

"Go ahead and stay. You don't have to be here in the morning," said Fox, without hesitation.

"Yeah...but what do I tell The Boss?"

"Just get in the limo with him, go to the airport, don't say anything unless he asks and, when you get to the airplane ramp, say goodbye!"

He made it sound so simple. No wonder he was laughing.

I pondered the advice. But all I had to do was look into Ann's blue eyes to know what had to be done—exactly what Fox had suggested.

When we got to the airport, Mulroney climbed one step, then turned around, noticing I was just standing there, immobile, on the tarmac.

"Are you coming back?" he asked.

"No sir. I think I'll stay behind with the boys..."

He didn't buy it for a second. He gave me that sarcastic Mulroney smirk, and said, "Another sacrifice for the country, eh?"

He turned and went inside the plane, while I breathed a sigh of relief. Later, he would tell the story that I had stayed behind, after we went to a Baie Comeau reception that was "full of pretty girls." He actually thought that was hilarious.

When I had to come back the next morning on a Buffalo military cargo aircraft, sitting in a net, I wasn't too sure the whole thing was such a good idea after all.

As for Mulroney's success with women in his bachelor days, most of what I've heard comes from his friends, who are still in awe of his Don Juan talents. All he told me himself was that, in his day, he was doing quite well.

One Montrealer, who knows him well, told me, "He used to go out with the most beautiful women in Montreal."

One of those was named Marie Fay. She was a Eurasian beauty, who Brian once escorted to a Montreal party, impressing every male present.

So far, so good. But no one, least of all Mulroney, was expecting Marie Fay to resurface after he became prime minister.

All was relatively quiet in the press office, when somebody phoned to say that some woman was talking about her relationship with Brian Mulroney, in a weekly Quebec gossip magazine.

I must have turned white. My God! That was all we needed. What was she saying? Nobody seemed to know.

Close to panic, I ordered my assistant, Sunni Locatelli, to find a copy of the darned magazine, anyway she could. This was a priority.

She came back with it about an hour later. I cringed when I saw a picture of the woman on the front page, with a headline about how she'd had a relationship with Brian Mulroney. Nervously, I turned to the inside pages and read the article.

I couldn't help but call in members of my staff, to

read aloud the part where she talked about going to a cottage in the Laurentians with Mulroney.

"He was always a perfect gentleman," she said. "I would sleep in the room, and he would sleep on the couch."

That was as bad as it got. Relieved, but with mischief in mind, I then proceeded to phone The Boss himself, and break the news.

"Mister Prime Minister," I said, as he took the call, "there's this woman that claims to have known you in your bachelor days. She gave an interview to a Quebec magazine."

I waited for a reaction, but all I could hear was the frantic chewing of his nicotine gum at the other end. Snickering, I went on to read him the "bad part." I could hardly finish before I burst out laughing.

Feigning indignation, he shouted, "It's true!" and started to laugh himself. He then asked to see a copy of the magazine, and asked how the woman, whom he hadn't seen in a number of years, looked.

Some will find many devious motives for Brian Mulroney to try and keep his past, as he says, where it is. I personally believe it has a lot to do with his children. He doesn't necessarily think that the kind of life he led before getting married is a good example. Remember, he put the family unit on his list of most important things, in his first Throne Speech.

He once told me he quit smoking because he didn't want to be a bad example for his kids. Anytime he would light up a cigarette, a TV camera would come on, or a photographer would be watching, and he didn't want to be perceived as a smoker by his family. It was tougher to quit that than alcohol and, still today, he likes people smoking around him—as long as it's not excessive—because he likes the smell of the burning cigarette.

But of all the things he tried to hide, the most serious one, to him, had nothing to do with his past. It was merely a human weakness—his fear of heights.

While I was there, it was actually a little more than that. Not only did he have a phobia about high places, but he had trouble standing in an open area with nothing in front of him—like a podium, for instance—without feeling like falling forward.

I never thought it was a big deal, as such. We could always work around it. But our biggest problem was trying to find ways to tell organizers of events that the prime minister wouldn't do certain things, without giving any explanation as to why. It was hard for them to understand, for instance, why the riser he was to speak on could not be more than six inches high.

The worst thing that was ever proposed to us, in that sense, happened at a curling bonspiel in Kitchener. Mulroney was scheduled to open the event. The organizers had a stage made to look like a huge curling rock. Several people could stand on it and, of course, they wanted the PM to do exactly that.

Now, that wasn't too bad, when the rock was on the ice. But the plan was to start the show with it hanging from the ceiling, about fifty feet above the ice, and slowly lower it, while all the time twirling the damn thing. To get to it, the prime minister also had to walk some sort of a gangplank just as high above the solid ground.

"You wouldn't believe what they wanted him to do!" the advance man, Stu Murray, said to me, when he came back from his preparatory trip.

Well, the whole thing was crazy for just about anyone, but, for Mulroney, it was suicide.

I told the prime minister about it, once the event was over with. He didn't say a word, and just looked at me, stone-faced. I felt he didn't even like me to raise the subject, when I actually thought it was rather funny.

However, I discovered a remarkable change in the man, years later. That was in February of 1990, when the *Sun* assigned me to cover his trip to Mexico and Barbados.

On the trip between Mexico and the Caribbean island, he came to the back of the plane, to chat with the boys. As he came up to me, he asked how things had gone. I told him about my visit to the Pyramids of the Sun and the Moon, where Mila had also been.

I had climbed half-way to the top of the Sun Pyramid—the less steep of the two. As I explained, going up was tough enough, but coming back down, with no railing to hang on to, I had found pretty dizzying.

I also laughed, while telling him the story about how Mrs. Mulroney's longtime assistant, Bonnie Brownlee, had to come down the steps of the Moon Pyramid sitting down, because she was afraid to fall if she stood up.

I was shocked to hear Mulroney say, then, "Can you imagine what it would have been like for me?"

I was really dumbfounded. Three years earlier, he never would have said anything like that to a member of his staff, let alone a reporter. That was admitting a weakness.

I said to myself that maybe he was mellowing, after all. Maybe he was changing for the better and learning that people accept weaknesses in their leaders because, in a strange way, it makes them feel less inadequate themselves.

Maybe Brian Mulroney finally understands that his real personality is better than the cardboard, too-perfect figure he has been trying to sell.

Maybe.

# Chapter 12

A lot has been said and written about Brian Mulroney's fascination with the media. His love-hate relationship with members of the press, over the years, has intrigued the people who report on his actions on a daily basis—if only because he followed a prime minister, Pierre Trudeau, who didn't give a damn about the Press Gallery.

Long before he became prime minister, Mulroney had a string of buddies in the press. Among them were Bill Fox, whom he would hire as his press secretary, Ian L. MacDonald, whom he would hire as a speech writer, and Hubert Bauch, to whom he would send a case of Scotch on his fortieth birthday in payment of a bet.

Fox and MacDonald were still among his intimates at last count—although, like all of Mulroney's friends, they take their regular turn in the doghouse when they dare displease The Boss. Bauch was never quite that close to him. The two men don't exactly march to the same drummer. Hubie, as he is known to his friends, has a bohemian streak that makes him wear clothes, and behave in wild ways, that are not compatible with the kind of person a prime minister should associate with.

In his strange, ambivalent way, though, Mulroney likes Hubie, if only because of his tremendous writing talents and his cool, easy-going nature. When he sees him in a crowd, for instance, Mulroney will often walk over to Bauch and tell him, "You don't look like one of the locals..."

The prime minister has also developed new media "friendships," since he took power in 1984. That, of course, often depends on what a reporter or columnist says about him. He can only take so much criticism. He has a lot of admiration for *Sun* columnist Doug Fisher, he respects the impact of *The Globe and Mail*'s Jeffrey Simpson, he thinks the *Globe*'s Graham Fraser is one of the best reporters in the land, and he believes that the Presse Canadienne's Pierre April is "one of ours." (That may have something to do with the fact that April used to be an ace reporter for the defunct *Montreal-Matin*, a Union Nationale newspaper.)

During the 1988 campaign, when he didn't have anything to do, Mulroney would distract his entourage by giving a list of those he thought were the ten "most serious" journalists in Ottawa, both French and English. I didn't make that early list, but one of his aides would confide in me the following year that, to his great astonishment, I had made the prime minister's journalistic hit parade.

"I couldn't believe my ears," said the adviser.

I didn't know whether to laugh or cry.

The prime minister evidently also has his list of reporters he simply couldn't stand if they offered to shine his Guccis. For charitable reasons, I will not name them. In fact, the list is rather fluid. Some names regularly go on and off it.

Mulroney will despise a reporter for the strangest reasons. I remember one occasion in Montreal, when he was upset at a local journalist who had tried to scrum him.

"Did you see the hat he was wearing?" he asked me.

"What kind of reporter would wear a hat like that?"

It was a grey fedora. Kind of a nice hat, in fact.

I was at a loss for words—maybe because I owned a hat like that myself. I guessed then that what Mulroney really meant was, "How dare somebody speak to me without taking his hat off—especially when he's being rude."

Mulroney tries to pretend he doesn't care as much as he used to about what the media say about him. And it is true that he has appeared more relaxed on international trips, for instance, coming to chat at the back of the plane more often than he did during the first mandate.

He also likes to fool around. His latest gimmick—since the arduous trip that took him to Singapore, Malaysia (for the Commonwealth Summit) and Costa Rica in 1989—has been to erupt into the cabin with a 35mm camera in hand, and blind everybody in turn with the flash.

The funniest one he pulled, though, had to be during the 1988 campaign, when somebody coming from his private quarters on the plane emerged wearing a Brian Mulroney look-alike mask. When the man took the mask off, it was the prime minister himself. Anybody on acid would have freaked out.

But, for all his mellowing-out, Mulroney still asks almost daily, "what are the boys saying?" His press aides are expected to find out how some key members of the media have assessed his performance.

One typical encounter took place between former PMO Communications Director and CTV star commentator Bruce Phillips, and top CBC political correspondent David Halton.

After an event on the road, Phillips was doing his duty, and asked Halton what kind of treatment his boss was going to get on the news that night.

Using a typical journalistic expression to say it was a favourable piece, Halton said it was just "a blow job."

That night Phillips was watching the newscast with the prime minister. After they viewed Halton's report, the PM turned to his aide, and said, "If that's a blow job, I'd hate to be raped by those guys!"

But for all that's been said about Mulroney's obsession with the media, little is known about how difficult it can get when you're acting as his spokesman or communications adviser. As much as he craves press attention, the man is a walking contradiction when it comes to being open with the media. He is constantly on his guard and desperately tries to control information, even in the face of absurdity.

Consider the following anecdotes:

It was back in the early winter of 1986. The prime minister and I were in Edmonton, Alberta, where he had just taken part in an open line show.

For months, The Boss had been badgering me with a damned weekly "radio message" that he wanted to give. Time after time, when he was in one of his complaining moods, he'd say "What about my radio message? I asked Fox for that months ago. Where is it?"

That usually happened during one of his rants about how the members of his cabinet were telling him that the only problem the government had was a lack a good communications. That, in his mind, meant that Fox and I were at the heart of the problem.

Now, I knew that Fox had been working on the project for some time, although I had warned him against it. It sounded a bit too much like Ronald Reagan to me—since the US president and former radio commentator had a weekly message that sometimes made the headlines, depending on the chosen theme. Mulroney had already been criticized for his "presidential" style, and I thought this would only add fuel to the fire.

But Mulroney was adamant and Fox, while trying to keep the whole thing as confidential as possible (quite a feat on Parliament Hill), had indeed been getting everything set up for it. Now the whole thing sounded darned easy to Mulroney, but it wasn't exactly like pulling a rabbit out of a hat.

First, you had to make sure the message was written every week. And, as stupid as it may sound, that was far from automatic in the under-staffed Communications department. But the most important thing was to make sure the distribution was done professionally.

Fox had finally managed to strike a deal with an Ottawa company to do just that and, on the day we flew to Edmonton, everything was ready to go.

I got a phone call in my hotel room, from Sunni Locatelli, to tell me the press release announcing the weekly radio message was going out at noon, Ottawa time. I said that was fine, and thought to myself that The Boss would be mighty pleased to find out that he finally got his wish.

I forgot about it for a couple of hours. Mulroney did the radio show, and invited me to ride in the limousine with him on the way to the airport. That meant he wanted to know how well he'd done.

I sat down with him and, as I often did, I read back from the notes I had taken down, to tell him what I thought might turn up in the news.

I had a few other minor communications to make, then, as an afterthought, I said, "Oh yeah...the press release for your weekly radio message is going out at noon."

"What press release?"

"To announce your radio message. The one you've been asking about..."

All of a sudden he got very agitated, and the tone of his voice went up, as he almost yelled, "We don't need a press release! What do you mean, a press release? This is unacceptable! Stop it now!"

"Sir, we're in the car, on the highway..."

Absolutely shaken by his reaction, I looked at my watch. It was three minutes to ten. I had three minutes to stop the press release, assuming they had abided by the noon release in Ottawa.

In a desperate attempt to apease the storm, I told the RCMP driver that we needed to get to a phone urgently. As I said that, we happened to be passing a gas station.

The whole security motorcade made an abrupt turn, and the PM's limousine stopped in front of the garage. I rushed inside what looked like a small convenience store, flanked by RCMP officers.

As we burst in, the Mounties flashed their badges and took over the phone in front of a man—the owner I guess—and a startled pregnant woman.

I tried to explain, with the little time I had. "I'm with the prime minister's office, and we need the phone."

The place was so small, however, that anybody could hear what I was saying. The woman, obviously very impressed by the whole thing, offered to leave to allow me some privacy. I nodded, but I swear I didn't expect her and the man to go out in the freezing rain, to wait for me to finish this ridiculous call.

Sunni came on the line.

Crossing my fingers I asked, "Sunni, is the press release on the radio message out yet?"

"It's about to go."

"Don't ask me any questions, just stop it, now!"

"It may already be too late..."

"Sunni, our jobs might ride on this one. Tell Fox I'll explain later...and that I'm sorry."

I got back in the car and told Mulroney that I really didn't know if I'd caught it in time. He sulked all the way to the airport. When we got there, I phoned Ottawa again and confirmed two things: the press release hadn't gone out, and Fox was ready to kill someone.

People have, indeed, killed for less.

For all the harassment and the criticism he put us through on his damned radio message, when the time came to do it, Brian Mulroney backed down at the last second. Why? I never knew. He was just...like that. He never had a weekly radio message, and I never heard about it again, except from Fox. What he said about it all was unprintable.

Another good example of how difficult things can get in the Godfather's media universe has to do with the cursed transcripts. Those are transcripts of his press conferences, his radio and television appearances, scrums and, more importantly, private interviews.

The latter is where the prime minister usually makes

the mistake of thinking that his only audience is the person sitting down with him in the room. He seems to forget that the reporter listening to him will actually report what he hears and is almost always taping the conversation, meaning that there is an actual recording of it. As we found out often, it's hard to make a tape lie.

Mulroney had been burned early in the first mandate by such a transcript. It was a TV interview he had given, while still Opposition leader, to Hamilton open-line-show host Tom Cherington. Three years later, during my first book tour, I would myself go on Cherington's show and tell him how much aggravation he had caused with one question. That was when he had asked Mulroney if the taxpayers would have to pay for his "nanny" and his grocery bill, once he got to 24 Sussex.

" No, no," the righteous leader had said. "It seems to me there are a number of things like that, that have to be changed, that if you are to ask people to make sacrifices and to join you, then you have to provide the leadership—that's one area."

Mulroney had forgotten about the throw-away line, but the Canadian Press's dogged reporter, Edison Stewart, hadn't, and he had the transcript, provided by the leader's office, to back it up. In the first months of the mandate, he pursued the matter and embarrassed the press office and the prime minister in a big way with it, as I described in *"So, What Are the Boys Saying?"*

After that, the Boss was literally paranoid about transcripts—any transcripts. He wouldn't trust us to check them out before they went out. He would nervously ask to see each and every one of them, before publication. Sometimes, he'd spot something he didn't like, and simply relay the message that he didn't want the transcript to be made public. Most of the time, he wouldn't even tell us what bothered him with it.

As a result, I was often left trying to explain the unexplainable—that the PM's office could not even provide a transcript of an already-published interview. We couldn't say they weren't available. Everybody in the media knew we had them, since we would regularly defend ourselves by quoting from transcripts. So whenever one of the reporters would ask if we could provide him with a transcript, I would give some convoluted explanation as to how we didn't have the financial or human resources to do them all the time. When the request dealt with a private interview, I would refer them to the reporter who had actually done the interview. If he was willing to give them the tape, good for them. Often, I would cross my fingers, hoping the said reporter wouldn't provide it, or that the demander was too lazy or busy to listen to a one-hour tape.

Through it all, I always thought the whole thing was utterly ridiculous, and that The Boss was simply being picky, making mountains out of molehills. It reminded me of the guy who goes out to buy all the copies of a given newspaper, to make sure his parents don't see that he's made a total fool of himself, when the rest of the world knows. But I also knew very well of Mulroney's unfortunate tendency to hyperbole and, for that reason, I understood how important it was to clear all transcripts with him, if only to cover my ass. I told all members of my staff the same thing, since I was responsible for their actions and didn't want to be hung by them.

But, the harder you try to cover up, the more likely you are to slip up. So let me tell you about "the transcript that got away."

I was in Montreal with The Boss, in the winter of 1986. We were about to go to Washington for a return visit with Ronald Reagan, and Mulroney was granting interviews to the American media, to try and sell the Canadian line before the actual trip.

One of these interviews had been given to *The New York Times*, and my associate—and expert in international affairs—Marc Lortie was really gung-ho to put the transcript out. He called me at the Ritz-Carlton, to ask me about it. I hadn't read it yet so, in a quiet moment, I sat down in my room and did so.

The transcript was incredibly bad. It had a lot of spelling mistakes and contained pieces of conversation where Mulroney, for instance, was asking the reporter if he wanted sugar and cream in his coffee. I phoned Ottawa, to tell Lortie that he first had to clean that mess up, before releasing anything.

He did, and sent me a new copy over the fax machine, while telling me, all the time, that his damned transcript was ready to go. I sighed, wondering why Marc was so insistent about this. When I got the document, I brought it over to The Boss and nonchalantly asked him to review it, sure in my heart that there was nothing to it.

"Marc really wants this out before your visit to Washington," I said. "Would you mind looking it over?"

As I remember it, that was on a Friday, and we were spending most of the weekend in Montreal.

It didn't take long for The Boss to answer me. "I don't want that transcript out," he said. I think I asked him if he'd mind telling me why, but whether I did or not, I never got an explanation.

I phoned a dejected Lortie, to tell him the bad news.

"It was all ready to go, it was at the mail room," said Marc.

"Sorry buddy, he doesn't want it out. Make sure you get all the copies back...and destroy them!"

I felt bad for Marc, knowing how dedicated he was to the job. But I wasn't going to go against the prime minister, and have it blow up in my face later.

The weekend went by without incident. I was working quietly in my office on Monday morning when Sunni Locatelli walked in, with a worried look.

"Uh...I think the *New York Times* transcript went out," she said.

"What? But I told Marc..."

"Yeah, I know. I don't know what happened."

It wasn't even 10:00 a.m. yet. Maybe, I thought, it wasn't too late.

"Where is it?"

"The mail room tells me it went out at about 8:30 this morning. It's the first transcript, not the corrected version."

"Oh shit! that's even worse! He's gonna kill me...look, Sunni, maybe it's not too late. Phone the gallery right now, and try to get them back. Maybe we'll get lucky, and the clerks won't have taken the copies out of the box yet. It's Monday morning; they've got all the weekend stuff to clear up. Hurry!"

Twenty minutes later, she came back with triumphant news. "I got the box back!"

"Was it the only one that went out?"

"Yes."

"You sure?"

"Yes, but..."

"But what?"

"There was one copy missing."

My heart sank, as I asked, "Do they know who got it?"

"I asked the gallery clerks. They figure it must be the copy boy from Canadian Press, since he automatically takes all the releases as they arrive. He's just about the only one who does that."

"Canadian Press! Might as well give it to the world!"

CP being a wire service, any information it receives is transmitted to every newspaper, radio and TV station in the country.

Sure enough, it didn't take long before I got a phone call from my old friend, the transcript decoder, Edison Stewart. He had spotted a contradiction in the interview, having to do with Mulroney's version of events of the tuna scandal, in the fall of 1985, and the resulting resignation of Fisheries Minister John Fraser.

The prime minister was now saying, "Bang! I secured the minister's resignation..."

He had always said that Fraser had offered his resignation, and he had accepted it.

It was no big deal, I thought, but that was obviously what Mulroney himself had noticed while reviewing the transcript.

Stewart also wanted to know why he had the only copy available. There, I got lucky. Since the copies that had gone out were the unedited ones, I could just stall and say that all he had to do was read his own copy to realize that it was not fit for publication, since it was filled with mistakes.

Of course, I didn't tell him that another version had been all ready to go out since the previous Friday.

As for Mulroney, he was predictably delighted to look like a fool in the press, and be questioned by the opposition in the House about it. He was really proud of his press secretary.

All I could say in my defence was, "I gave the order. I don't know what happened."

I didn't even bother telling him that one box had mysteriously been forgotten in the Privy Council's mailroom, and that one zealous employee had made it his duty to deliver it as soon as he got in on Monday morning, not knowing that we had put a stop on it three days before.

Any explanation was pointless. I took my briefcase and returned to the doghouse for a prolonged stay.

In retrospect, as important as they seemed then, I'm convinced that these were really petty concerns for the prime minister, and that the only reason they took on greater proportions was that we were constantly getting caught trying to hide things. The members of the press were not blind. They knew it, and they knew it bugged Mulroney to the utmost when they went after him for something like a "contradiction."

All he had to say on the Fraser thing was that dealings between himself and his ministers were just that, and he didn't intend to discuss the details. Besides, among the public, who cared if Fraser was fired or resigned willingly?

He would have been better to shrug it off once in a while. It might have made his job, and everybody else's, a little easier.

Another aspect of being Brian's mouthpiece that can be rather frustrating is his tendency to arrange things without telling his press officers about them. Sometimes he'll book his own interviews. You'll get a call from some talk-show host in Montreal or Toronto, telling you that the prime minister promised him or her an interview, and it is expected to happen—now! You ask the prime minister about it and, more often than not, he acts as if he doesn't know what you're talking about. At first, you believe him. But, when it keeps happening over and over again, you start thinking that maybe the top guy's got a problem. As a spokesman, you're then stuck with trying to make an interview fit into an already-crowded schedule, or turning it down without hurting The Boss's reputation in the process. It can get hairy.

Then there was his worst habit, which was more common in the early days of his rookie mandate, when he would sometimes phone a reporter's superior to complain about a story or stories. For instance, he did it to Quebec columnist Michel Vastel, when he was working for Montreal's *La Presse*.

Those shenanigans didn't make our jobs in the press office easier, either, when the reporter found out about it. And, besides, they were useless.

It takes a hell of a lot for an editor to respond to that kind of criticism, even when it's coming from the prime minister. It's hard to know how often Mulroney did it. I suspect he often used his friends to carry his messages.

Then, there were also the deals and commitments he made with other leaders or politicians, without telling his press relations people about them.

Now, the prime minister does not have to tell his press secretary everything he does. But when it involves something that's bound to become public and is not controversial—unless you try to hide it—then, perhaps, he should give notice to the office that constitutes his first line of defence, and his window to the outside world.

Such a screw-up happened with Kelly.

Who's that? Kelly's a horse. He used to be a Canadian horse, but now he's an American. As a matter of fact, not just any American horse. Kelly has former president Ronald Reagan as his owner and master.

How did that happen? We're not sure...

Like the Creature from the Black Lagoon, it came from Washington. A lot of Canadian news comes out of the American capital, because the US is a lot more open about divulging our current affairs than we are ourselves. I was long gone from the PMO, but I was told the story by some incredulous insiders, who knew I would sympathize and understand what they had gone through.

The horse's story came out of the mouth of the head horse himself, good ol' Ronnie. This was in the final days of his presidency, in January of 1989. He was doing one of his countless, meaningless photo-ops, while receiving a beautiful western saddle as a parting gift. That was when Ronnie blurted out that the saddle would go well with the horse the Canadians were giving him.

It didn't take long for inquiries to start flooding the press office. This was in the interim period following the re-election, and the new press secretary had not been appointed yet. So, Communications Director Bruce Phillips was handling the calls. He didn't have a clue what they were talking about.

After doing the rounds, he finally found out that the horse had been promised by The Boss himself, in the course of a phone conversation with the president. But, for some reason, Mulroney had forgotten to follow up on the promise.

Now, the PMO had to find a horse!

In the meantime, all calls about the president's horse simply did not exist. The press office did not exist. Because the damned horse did not exist.

After scurrying around, it was finally decided that the horse would come from the RCMP's Musical Ride. That was how Kelly got the call.

The memo to the Privy Council—obtained through Access to Information by CBC Newsworld reporter Kirk Lapointe—read like this:

Name: Kelly
Number: PSH 630
Old: 1971
By: Halton
Out of: Joan
Black, 16 hands, 1,275 pounds
Description: Superb disposition, good confirmation, consistent performer, bold disposition with an inquisitive nature.

Yes, they actually wrote that the horse had an "inquisitive nature."

Now, that was hilarious enough for Phillips and his staff, who, by this time, had horse jokes coming out of their ears. But what provoked the greatest outburst of laughter was Kelly's age.

As one insider said, "We're not horse experts, but we know how to use a calculator."

He meant that, at eighteen, the horse was ninety years old, in human terms.

"We've given him a swayback!" shouted Phillips. "This horse is older than the president!"

As it turned out, Kelly was apparently the perfect horse to give as a gift, and adapted very well to its new surroundings—including the western saddle.

But the PMO did get a scare when, a few weeks later, they learned that Ronald Reagan had fallen from his horse. Oh no! Kelly had thrown the president! It turned out to be another equine culprit.

Nevertheless, the story of Kelly The Horse will go down as another typical Mulroneyism.

If the reader finds all of this a little befuddling and confusing, be thankful. At least you don't work for the guy. When you see the glum figure of a press secretary lurking in the background on your TV screen, when you read a stupid quote from a prime minister's "spokesman" in the newspaper, be gentle. Say a little prayer.

# Chapter 13

What kind of a boss was The Boss? You can't answer that question without considering the fact that Brian Mulroney, in only six years, has had under his command three drastically different teams, with very few veterans staying in for the long haul.

That is both a measure of the inexperience of a rookie prime minister—and his equally inexperienced staff—and of a management style that makes Mulroney get rid of, and replace, people once they have served their purpose, as you change the deck of cards at the table when the luck isn't going your way. It is also symptomatic of a place where you live out your usefulness and effectiveness very quickly. You grow old and helpless fast.

Almost always, when comes the changing of the praetorian guard, it must be said that discarded staffers are "taken care of." They are either rewarded with good apppointments—a few of them get the overseas plums—or they are promised by The Boss that he will not forget them.

The three Mulroney PMO

regimes can be easily identified: it started with the "cronies." They lasted a little more than the first half of the initial mandate. That was followed by the Derek Burney bureaucratic regime that pulled him through the election. And finally came what I call "the aftermath," a group of people Mulroney seems to care less and less about.

Two things, above all, will always stick in my mind and my heart about working for Brian Mulroney. First, how he makes you feel that you were nobody and nothing, until he pulled you out of the gutter and granted you the honour of working for him. Second, how he can love you one day and ignore you the next.

The management style that makes him dump certain members of his staff, when they become more of a liability than an asset, is also reflected in his day-to-day contacts with them. I'm not speaking of the bureaucracy. I'm talking about the "political" or, as the bureaucrats have designated those pariahs, the "exempt" staff who serve "at will." The expression means the prime minister can get rid of you on a whim, like a member of his cabinet.

Mulroney's PMO is like a big parking lot. A lot of people sit in their offices as though they are waiting at a red light that never changes. In time, they start wondering what they're doing there, why the prime minister doesn't phone, why they're not being asked to do anything significant. Usually, if this state of suspended animation lasts long enough, the proudest individuals will start complaining and making noises about leaving. That's when they mysteriously start getting calls from the prime minister. All of a sudden, their opinion is valuable again.

Mulroney will then pretend to discuss with you every problem under the sun, and make you feel that you are a crucial part of the solution.

That's a crock, of course. He is merely playing the game of charm that he is a master at. Why? Because he doesn't want that individual to leave. He wants him to be there for the day he needs him, down the road. He is, of course, the only person to know what that day is.

Could be for the next election, or the next speech. But he knows, like no other, how to put the pressure on to keep you there.

If you still resist his will and pray to be let go, then look out. You quickly become a non-person and a traitor to the cause. He freezes you out. He doesn't ask you how your wife and kids are anymore, he doesn't even say hello, let alone seek your advice on national matters.

Believe me. Just about everybody who went through there knows that this is true.

I was part of the first wave, "the cronies." And if anybody, among the nice bunch of people I worked with then, owes a lot to Brian Mulroney, paradoxically, it's probably me. Yet, I'm one of the rare ones who defied him and didn't get a job or a reward—although he tried to make me believe my severance pay was one—after I left.

I owe him a lot for the simple reason that I managed to cut the ties. That's not easy with a man whose power rests largely on the strength of his network of "friends" across the country. He doesn't like those who get away from his sphere of influence. He truly expects them to be there forever. It's all a matter of gratitude.

But I was lucky—incredibly lucky—to bounce back. Not too many people cross the Godfather and live to tell about it. I came back somewhat through the rear door, when he wasn't looking.

As one staffer told me recently, "When you left the PMO and went back to *Le Droit* (a struggling paper with a 40,000 circulation), his thoughts must have been, 'That's all Gratton was ever good for anyway...'"

He then let his guard down and forgot what a bothersome fly I was. Of course, he wasn't expecting that, only a little more than a year later, I'd be staring him in the face from the other side of the fence, writing a national column for one of the biggest newspaper chains in the country.

The first book helped, of course. But it was really the expertise I had acquired inside the halls of power, coupled with the fact that I was willing to share it with the world, that made the difference. In that sense, I have to say to Brian Mulroney: Thanks a million. You were right. I'd be nowhere without you.

It was Bill Fox who told me, on more than one occasion, that Mulroney liked to believe that "he made each and every one of us."

Fox, in particular, hated that. After all, the man was the Washington correspondent for *The Toronto Star*, the biggest paper in the country, before Mulroney begged him to come and work in Ottawa. He didn't feel he owed anything to Brian Mulroney, other than the aggravation the job brought.

And what about Bernard Roy? He took a pay cut to leave his law practice and come to Ottawa, against his better judgement. Things were so bad financially at one point that the chief-of-staff and principal secretary to the prime minister confided in me that his wife might have to go find work. Does that sound to you like someone who's been handed the key to heaven?

Bernard was never one to complain, however. His former roomate, Brian, whom he called "Mr. Prime Minister" in front of other people, needed him. He genuinely considered the job a great honour, and I believe he toughed it out for almost four years simply to prove to himself and others that he could do it. He also played a key role in negotiating the Meech Lake Accord, no small accomplishment.

Fox and Roy were considered "cronies," and suffered unfairly from the label. But no one was hurt more by it than senior adviser Fred Doucet. For some reason that had more to do with perception than fact, Fred was immediately branded a bumbling incompetent by the Ottawa media. He was the ultimate example of cronyism. Doucet's only real mistake was that he shouldn't have dealt with the media publicly. In fact, he was one of the main reasons Mulroney enjoyed success on the international scene since, for the first three crucial years, he was in charge of every major international venture, both at home and overseas.

If anybody was used by Mulroney, it had to be Fred—although he would never admit that himself. He paid for his dedication to the job with a massive heart attack, prior to the second election campaign. That was after The Boss had already shoved him aside.

Another "crony" was former St. Francis Xavier University friend Pat MacAdam. Between 1980 and 1983, while working for Tory MPs on the Hill, he did the dirty work of discrediting Joe Clark, in order to eventually replace him with his champion. He did such a good job that Mulroney hired him as his "caucus liaison" man.

That was his official title. "Hit man" would have been more accurate. MacAdam continued to do in power what he had done in opposition; cause trouble for the opposition, wherever it may be, and act as The Boss's personal terrorist.

The point to all this is that, when the media said Mulroney had given jobs to his friends to thank them for their services, they had it backwards. The Boss surrounded himself with people he knew and had faith in because, at the time, that is what he wanted and needed.

You have to remember that he didn't know who to trust, as he took the reins of power after twenty-two years of uninterrupted Grit rule (except for the nine-month Clark interval). He firmly believed, like most of us, that the bureaucracy had been largely politicized at the highest echelons by the Trudeau regime, and that a conspiracy of bureaucratic eggheads and key members of the media was already plotting to overthrow the Tory rule.

He needed time to feel his way around, and his faithful team provided him with the buffer he wanted. He also knew that his blindly loyal troops would obey just about any order, to make sure he succeeded.

In time, members of the PMO, like myself, Fox, Doucet and Roy would take a good part of the rap for the mistakes of the first three years in power. With hindsight, I can now say that, for all our setbacks, we weren't all that bad; more often than not, we simply obeyed the orders of the man we were paid to help and, above all, re-elect. Were we yes-men? Perhaps we just believed a little too much. Charm, especially the Mulroney charm, can make you do a lot of things you wonder about later. It's a little like reviewing your actions after a crazy drunk.

As one shrewd observer of the political scene, who has also been on both the inside and the outside, told me, "What I have found about people who get into politics is that they lose their sense of balance."

He was right on. When you become directly involved in a cause, winning becomes the only thing. Squares somehow fit into circles, because you make them fit. The truth depends on the weather.

The biggest mistake one can make, when judging the performance of any given PMO, is to think that ideas and policies actually emanate from there. Nothing could be further from the truth.

Oh, there are a few idealists or advisers in the prime minister's praetorian guard, who like to believe that they actually have a big word to say in the future of the country, and there is no doubt that some, like Bernard Roy on Meech Lake, do contribute to a given dossier.

But, by and large, the PMO's power is a myth. It is exactly the opposite of how people on the outside picture it. Any thinker quickly becomes a plumber in there. Perhaps fireman would be a more appropriate word, since a good part of the working day is taken up putting out fires. You don't have much time to think when the house is burning.

The key jobs are not necessarily the top ones. The positions that have anything to do with the way the prime minister is perceived in the outside world are the ones that count. In that sense, his executive assistant, the press office, Communications, the tour office, and the legislative adviser who briefs the PM daily on the questions he may face in the Commons are the most important, along with the little-known correspondence unit—those are the people who answer the mail, and sign Brian Mulroney's name at the bottom. But most of the work they accomplish is very short-term, if not urgent and immediate.

The only events you can actually plan and almost

control are the public outings and the international trips. But, as we'll see later, even those seem to go awry on a disconcertingly regular basis for Mulroney.

What I mean to say is that most people are so caught up in the day-to-day operation of the place that they don't have much time to think about the government's vision of the country. The Prime Minister's Office is not a place for ideas to germinate and grow.

In our case, it was also as close as we could come to a Tower of Babel. Everybody was talking at the same time, and nobody understood each other. In-fighting for influence was a daily occurrence. And a lot of people who should have been working to achieve the same goals were actually spending a lot of time trying to destroy each other.

That reality, as much as anything else, contributed to the image of incompetence that plagued Brian Mulroney's first PMO.

Bernard Roy was a tolerant man—too tolerant for this bunch. He permitted an inordinate amount of access to The Boss from too many people in the PMO. It is difficult to imagine how he could have done otherwise under the circumstances, though. Because, very often, Mulroney himself was to blame for the excessive access he provided to too many people.

The communications went both ways, as The Boss thought it was perfectly normal for him to phone up and chat with individual members of his staff, without going through the normal chain of command. Most of the time, his calls were designed more to find out what was going on within his office or elsewhere in town, than to seriously deal with government policy.

He wanted to know everything that was going on. He understood that a man's power depended largely on the amount and quality of the information he had about the world around him.

As an example, take this exchange I once had with former minister Lucien Bouchard, when we had dinner shortly after the 1988 election campaign. At the time, I was still very high on Mulroney's blacklist.

"I didn't tell him I was meeting you tonight," he said.

"It's probably better that way," I answered.

"He'll find out, don't worry," replied the longtime friend, who knew The Boss well. "He finds out everything."

He chuckled after saying that, and I could guess that thoughts of Brian's obsession with knowing what's going on were going through his mind.

"You're right, he does."

Another thing Mulroney would do with several of his staffers was tell them to transmit orders he should have given himself.

How many times did he tell me, for instance, "I want you to tell Bernard to do this?"

That always made me feel very uncomfortable. I couldn't say no to the prime minister, and if I wavered, he made me feel like a wimp for not following his orders. But then I found it really unusual, not to say unacceptable, that I, the employee, should tell my chief-of-staff what to do. But Mulroney seemed to think it was perfectly normal.

At least in my case, the relationship was strictly professional, although it is true that he often treated me more like his son than his staffer. But for others, like Fox, Doucet, policy adviser Charley McMillan, and speech writer Ian MacDonald—to name but a few—there was the added dimension of being a personal friend. That, for Mulroney, made the contacts between him and them even more normal, no matter if he short-circuited his chief-of-staff in the process. And, let's face it, those who got the phone calls were happy to feel that the prime minister valued their opinions—myself included.

But it resulted in a lot of internal power struggles. Who was going to sit next to The Boss? Who would he be phoning for advice that night?

I always suspected Mulroney knew this. And over the years, as I observed, from both the inside and the outside, the way he dealt with his staff, it became quite evident to me that he deliberately divided to reign.

For instance, he intentionally left doubt in my mind

and Fox's as to who was running the press office, when I replaced Bill as press secretary, and he became director of communications. When things aren't clear, clashes occur, creating confusion and bad feelings. He appointed Fred Doucet senior adviser, then gave a similar title to Charley McMillan, prompting Fred to ask if he was number one or not. He angered Fox by appointing Ian Anderson "deputy chief-of-staff," meaning he was in charge when Bernard Roy wasn't there (Anderson, another former reporter, and Fox didn't really get along professionally). When Fox expressed his dissatisfaction, the PM told him that Anderson would merely be "pushing paper." Yet, he did have the title and the responsibilities. What was the truth?

Whatever it was, it existed clearly only in Brian Mulroney's complex mind. And I have come to believe that he liked it that way. Because it didn't stop with us. Those who followed, suffered a similar fate.

But I'm getting slightly ahead of myself.

There were also those who used the prime minister's name in vain. "The Boss wants this, The Boss wants that." In fact, they wanted it, and had never discussed it with Mulroney. But they gambled on the hope that Mulroney would never find out they were using his authority, since it was doubtful that I, for instance, would ask him directly if it was true. Needless to say, when such schemes did become known, again tempers would flare up in the PMO, and cooperation would cease between people and departments who depended on each other to do their jobs.

While I was there, this was not only a problem for the prime minister inside the government. There were several instances of Tories on the outside who would claim to be "friends of Brian," to get favours or advantageous commercial deals. In fact, Mulroney has, justifiably, almost become paranoid about it. Whenever he hears—even today—that one of his so-called friends has used his name to garnish his wallet, he intervenes to put an end to it. In many instances, to be a friend of the prime minister has become a liability.

This was more true in the early years than it is now. It was then fuelled in the media by the seemingly unending string of scandals that plagued the regime. The press was seeing crooked Tories behind every shady transaction, especially in Quebec. After a while, Mulroney learned to control those hustlers on the outside a little better, as he put the fear of God in them. But he is still extremely vigilant about it, probably because he believes, rightly, that the media would rather feast on another good scandal than believe his denials.

The first PMO, although headed by Bernard Roy, one of the most honest and straightforward persons I have met in politics, was also continuously under suspicion. The cloak of corruption seemed to stain everybody. The closer you were to Mulroney, the more vulnerable you became. The press watched us like hawks. Vultures would probably be a better word.

As a result, we became probably the most famous—or was it infamous?—group of prime ministerial aides in modern times. We were stars, all right. But none of it was good.

At some point during my tenure, there was even a joke going around Ottawa about us. It went, "What's the difference between Rock Hudson's and Brian Mulroney's aides?"

Answer: "Mulroney's aides haven't killed him yet."

In the end, he eliminated us.

In the spring of 1987, with the appointment of Derek Burney as chief-of-staff, the PMO made a 180 degree turn in every aspect.

As one staffer described it to me, "Burney was everything. He was the press secretary. He was the director of communications. He was the tour director. He controlled the whole machine."

Bernard Roy, by then, had retained only the title of principal secretary, something he confided in me he was very happy with. It meant that he could work on dossiers like Meech Lake, without having to worry about the day-to-day administration of the office. It also meant he had virtually lost all his power, but kept his unique influence on the prime minister. He was later replaced by another Mulroney Laval buddy, Peter White, who made a comeback to the PMO he had left two years before to go work for Conrad Black's empire. White kept a low profile during this second coming.

Burney was a very intimidating man for almost everybody who worked under him. One hard-nosed aide confided, to my great surprise, "The prime minister doesn't intimidate me. But Burney certainly does!"

Another told me the story of how he walked into the chief-of-staff's office one day to see him wearing a baseball cap and swinging a baseball bat menacingly, as he dictated a memo to his secretary. The aide was quite impressed.

Actually, the man was just an avid baseball fan and part-time player. But the bat-wielding image fit. And it fed the legend of the chief-of-staff who ate nails for breakfast. In fact, Burney was probably more a shrewd and experienced operator, who didn't care what it took to do his job.

At the time of the Toronto Economic Summit in June 1987, Mila's executive assistant casually asked him, "Derek, are you going to bring your wife?"

"Why?" replied a baffled Burney. "We're working."

I wasn't surprised by the exchange. I recalled how he used to work his External Affairs staff into the ground on international trips, when I was travelling with the prime minister. Often, his people would literally work right through the night, preparing documents or speeches. I remember thinking at the time that he was merciless, and that I didn't envy those who worked under him.

Personally, I got along great with him. He had a sparkle in his eye and a wicked sense of humour. He was tough, all right, but "no-nonsense" would probably describe him better. The fact that he couldn't order me around certainly made the relationship easier. That obviously wasn't the case for the people I left behind in the PMO.

Burney was well-served by his vast bureaucratic experience. He knew the way Ottawa worked, both at home and abroad, since he'd been given several diplomatic postings. He knew which strings to pull to get his way.

For example, when I was there, one of the most difficult things to arrange seemed to be salary increases. The bureaucracy always appeared to make it extremely complicated, if not impossible. But they couldn't bullshit Burney. He was one of them, and he knew how to use his power to get the things he wanted.

When the prime minister told him he wanted Luc Lavoie in the PMO to help his communications strategy, especially in Quebec, Burney set up a meeting with the prospective employee. Lavoie, a former TV journalist and whiz kid, barely thirty years of age, was minister Marcel Masse's chief-of-staff. He was flattered by the call to the PMO, but he liked Masse both professionally and personally. He didn't really want to leave for the uncertain world of Brian. So, when Burney came to him, he asked for an almost outrageous salary that came dangerously close to six figures.

To his astonishment, the PM's envoy simply said, "You've got it."

Lavoie was on board, and contributed greatly to the TV success of the following campaign. However, before the campaign actually came along, he spent some long and lonely times in his PMO office, waiting to do something, other than go to boring, useless meetings and wonder why he was there. Like a pinch-hitter in baseball, though, he was expected to produce when called upon to do so, as he did for Lucien Bouchard's by-election, three months before the real contest.

Burney also knew that his only chance for success was to clean the shop as much as he could, and bring in his own people from other government departments. The key move in that strategy was, as I said earlier, to get rid of powerful and influential Bill Fox. He brought in his own assistant, and got together a secretarial pool that was at least double the size of Bernard Roy's.

Marc Lortie, the press secretary who was also still officially an External Affairs employee, became an ally of

Burney's because he quickly understood the power of the man.

Everything was now truly run by "the second floor" of the Langevin building. The rest of the staff were hit by the "plumbers' syndrome" more than ever before. Burney ran the show with his people, and couldn't have cared less about the rest, as long as they didn't get out of line, or try to discuss important matters with the prime minister without his prior approval.

That, however, did not stop the trench warfare within the office. Lortie and Phillips, for instance, were at odds for practically the whole time they worked together—or was it against each other? They did not become friends, or even allies.

It's hard to understand how that happened between two highly intelligent and sensitive human beings. But it was, in part, Mulroney's fault. When he asked Phillips to come to Ottawa to take on the Director of Communications job, he left him with the impression that he was running everything, including the press office. When he appointed Lortie press secretary, there seemed to be no doubt, for the appointee, that he actually ran his shop and was the official spokesman.

Yet, on many occasions, such as the conclusion of the Meech Lake Accord, it was Phillips who ended up breaking the news to the media and fielding reporters' questions. Phillips also used to write most of the press releases.

He also created some problems for himself—perhaps stemming from jealousy—when, partly because of his national TV image, he developed a very high profile. That was a no-no Mulroney wanted to avoid, after our disastrous attempt at celebrity.

Lortie was more laid-back and less prone to inflammatory statements. Eventually his approach won out, because it was a low-risk one. Phillips insisted on staying through the election campaign, because his sense of honour dictated it. In time, he became another Mulroney casualty, when he finally served out his usefulness. His greatest quality, through it all, was that he knew exactly what made the media tick, and he would always give the prime minister the score, no matter how hard it was. Mulroney squeezed the advice out of him, then squeezed him out of his office by appointing him Privacy Commissioner. Another man in the network.

The Boss also conned Lortie, a career bureaucrat, into staying on as press secretary for the election campaign. That was a ruthless, uncaring move. Had he been defeated, Lortie would have been blackballed just about everywhere in the public service. In fact, he suffered from his association with Mulroney even after the victory, when he was appointed to the number two position in Canada's embassy to France. The career diplomats froze him out for months afterwards. Imagine how it would have been if Mulroney had lost.

But what Brian wants, Brian gets. If he wants to hang himself, everyone else should do the same thing. If he doesn't take holidays, everybody should work.

Like a senior aide who, at one point, said he was going on a two-week holiday, when Mulroney was going through a particularly rough period. The Boss complained openly that this ungrateful employee was going away for "two months." Even when corrected, he went on talking about "two months," as if he hadn't heard.

Gambling on Lortie's career, because he couldn't find a suitable replacement for the campaign, was only par for the course. But he sent Lortie to Paris, and Derek Burney was appointed ambassador to Washington—although he took the precaution of making the official announcement before the election campaign, Burney didn't go until after.

Two more Mulroney contacts and loyalists in crucial embassies. The Boss's web grows ever bigger and reaches ever farther.

Was Burney a true Murloneyite, or was he just a bureaucrat without political affiliation or conviction, briefly seconded to rescue a sinking ship?

Let's just say that, when my former girlfriend, Ann Charron, was being considered as one of the secretaries on Mulroney's campaign plane, it was Burney who intervened. A dejected Ann was told that Burney had laid down the law, saying she couldn't be part of the team when I was also on the plane as a reporter. What did a simple bureaucrat have to do with Mulroney's campaign aircraft?

Burney left Mulroney with one piece of advice, concerning the choice of his new PMO staff after the November 21 triumph. "Take your time. You've got all the time in the world."

He did.

He appointed Stanley Hartt as his chief-of-staff soon after the vote. Hartt, another Mulroney friend and Montreal lawyer, had previously been given the pivotal job of Deputy Minister of Finance by the prime minister. He had resigned before the campaign, but Mulroney had managed to lure him back with the more prestigious PMO plum. The prime minister thought he was perfect for the job, given the fact that, on top of being a loyal friend and partisan, he had also acquired some experience in the bureaucracy for a couple of years.

But if Hartt's appointment came early, the PMO then seemed to grind to a halt. The press secretary's job, for instance, was not filled for several weeks. Mulroney's window to the world remained closed, as the prime minister "took his time."

In fact, it didn't make much difference to the outside world. The earth did turn a few times without additional pain or discomfort. But the boys and girls from the Press Gallery were getting restless. When the appointment finally came, it was a shocker: Mulroney had hired another journalist, veteran *La Presse* political reporter Gilbert (not Luc) Lavoie. More surprising was the fact that Lavoie had taken a sabbatical from his newspaper to come to the PMO—meaning that his job as a journalist was assured, if he quit politics within a reasonable time.

Within the PMO and the Ottawa journalistic community, people were shocked by the fact that a reporter would not cut his ties with his employer before jumping to the other side of the fence.

But if, for Lavoie, it was merely a way to ensure that he wasn't left on the street, unable to support his family, for the prime minister it was a clear indication that the press secretary would not be admitted to his intimate circle. Since he'd already suffered through one reporter who had left to write a book about him, it was doubtful he would give access to a second mole. He probably heard, too, that, as he left *La Presse*, Gilbert Lavoie was told by his colleagues that he "could write a book," when he got out. Mulroney surely knew this.

Stanley Hartt, meanwhile, had another problem; the other Lavoie, Luc.

When he took the chief-of-staff's job, Burney apparently told him that the only way to succeed was his way. Wipe the slate and start anew with your own people.

He was very much intent on doing exactly that. But Mulroney made it difficult, if not impossible, for him. He made Luc Lavoie an untouchable.

Luc had been extremely effective staging media events during the campaign. Mulroney was impressed by his style, his strong instincts and his forcefulness. In many ways, Lavoie resembled the prime minister. When things got tough, he simply brought out the shotgun.

Mulroney told Hartt, "He stays."

He was counting on him especially for his international trips, and events at home. But, always thinking twenty chess moves ahead, he wanted Lavoie for the next election. All he had to do was keep him well-fed and happy for four years in the PMO stable.

That threw Stanley's plan off the rails. It meant two things. Lavoie could practically get what he wanted, and he had privileged access to The Boss, with the influence that came with it.

Luc was also now considered to be a veteran, and had allies within the office that Stanley didn't necessarily have, among them Mulroney's executive assistant, Rick Morgan.

The young Morgan, despite his youth and the fact that Mulroney hired him fresh out of university, had gained The Boss's absolute confidence. Brian had come to depend on him totally and, being with the prime minister almost twenty-four hours a day, the executive assistant controlled the agenda a lot more thoroughly than his title suggested. Remember that name. He's going places.

Lavoie won the first skirmish with Hartt, by imposing a drastic restructuring of the PMO, in which he became adviser for special events. That meant that he controlled Mulroney's public outings, in the country and abroad. He took over the Tour department, and took the press advance section out of the press office. As a result, the press office lost one of its crucial, if not its main, functions, media logistics.

The press secretary was no longer a spokesman, just a smokescreen and a buffer between Mulroney and the media. If he knew nothing about the substance or the logistics, he couldn't get in trouble.

As insignificant as it may have seemed to the outside world, this restructuring, approved by Mulroney, was vital to his new strategy, which was designed to keep the media at bay and facilitate his control of the agenda. The prime minister now wanted to do his own press relations. No more unreliable intermediaries.

Meanwhile, Luc Lavoie would be in the know, but wouldn't talk to reporters. The plan worked. After a while, the media simply stopped phoning the press office for anything but scheduling questions, and the press secretary rarely got himself or Mulroney in hot water.

But through it all, Stanley Hartt never had control of his office because, deliberately, The Boss had divided to reign.

It's nice to see that some things never change.

# Chapter 14

I just can't help it. The man makes me laugh. Brian Mulroney is such a total paradox that it's genuinely funny.

Most of those who have been close to him for any relatively long period of time, as I was for three years, end up having the same reaction, sooner or later. In many almost-lovable ways, he is a caricature of himself.

Brian is a walking contradiction, and it's difficult to determine which one is his real personality, the public or the private. Or is it a bit of both? Maybe, like an actor who has been typecast in a role, he has started to live out the part of politician and prime minister, to the point where what he thinks he should be to the outside world has infringed on the boy from Baie Comeau who made it big in Montreal.

William Shatner is more Captain Kirk than himself. Lorne Greene was Ben Cartwright. Ed Asner became Lou Grant.

Consequently, it's hard to figure out when he's being sincere. In fact, it may be that even the put-ons are sincere with him. He has elevated exaggeration to the level of normal behaviour. He doesn't even know he's doing it anymore.

How can the same man have so much class, and be so petty? How can he be so vengeful, and yet so sensitive to others? How can he like to be served and pampered, and give so much of himself? How can he be so brilliant politically, but appear so devious? How can he hold his principles dear, yet abuse his power? How can he survive as prime minister and have such a thin skin?

In the end, I have come to believe that Brian Mulroney is very much like a chameleon. He adapts to his surroundings. He is, above all, a practical man, rather than an intellectual one. He does what he thinks has to be done to survive. He prefers getting results over winning an argument. But his attempts at conciliation are often misconstrued as indecision and lack of personal convictions. As a result, his above-average intellect does not come across. He is not a thinker, he's a doer.

He would like to be known as someone with a superior intelligence but, for all his vindictiveness, he doesn't have the mean streak necessary to humiliate his less gifted adversaries, as Pierre Trudeau was prone to do. He likes to get even, but he doesn't enjoy hurting people, or seeing people get hurt.

Perhaps the best example of that was his private reaction to Greg Weston's book on John Turner, *Reign of Error*. He didn't mind that the Grit leader was being savaged, for a change. He'd had to suffer from it a bit himself the previous year, with the release of Claire Hoy's *Friends in High Places* and, to a lesser degree, with my book.

He didn't like, however, the personal attacks on Turner. Nobody could be all that bad. But most of all, he thought the treatment Turner's wife, Geills, got in the book was absolutely disgusting. And untypically, he let it be known to quite a few people.

Anybody who knows The Boss wouldn't be surprised by such a strong reaction. For all his sensitivity to criticism, he has always understood that, as a prominent public person, he is fair game. But he has never accepted his wife and family being hurt publicly because of him.

As one aide says, "If anybody attacks Mila, he takes out the shotgun!"

I didn't need that person to tell me that. I had seen his protective instincts first-hand, and I knew that even Mila herself couldn't calm him down when it happened.

It didn't matter to the prime minister that his strategists—those from party headquarters in particular—loved to use Mila for public and political events. Or that she had an office and staff, paid for by the taxpayers. That made her a legitimate target for some media columnists. But Brian felt that he was solely responsible for putting her through political hell, and that she shouldn't pay because certain people wanted to get to him.

Take, for instance, his reaction to the incident in Moncton, New Brunswick, in the spring of 1988, when his wife was injured as the couple and their bodyguards tried to fight their way through a crowd of demonstrators. Mila was hit in the stomach and hurt slightly. The police, despite a thorough investigation that included the careful study of video tapes of the incident, could never figure out how or by whom. As a matter of fact, there are some who firmly believe that she was actually struck accidentally by one of the bodyguards. If that was the case, though, there was little chance the police would dare reveal their findings, after the show Brian put on right after it happened.

When scrummed by the journalists, Mulroney made it sound as if his wife had been beaten to a pulp by what he described as "a giant of a man...wielding a big stick."

I remember thinking at the time, *There he goes again...* I couldn't understand why the prime minister wasn't letting the incident speak for itself. He looked like he was trying to exploit his wife's misfortune to boost himself. And, on top of it all, he was blowing out of proportion an incident that may have been unpleasant and slightly scary, but that was relatively minor. The country's cartoonists had a field day.

What didn't dawn on me at the time was that he probably wasn't faking it. He was simply being totally irrational because his wife, not he, had been hurt. Since he is given to hyperbole when he has full control of his faculties, I guess we shouldn't be surprised if he really pours it on when he loses it.

His constant tendency to magnify things, to make them, or himself, seem more important, is perhaps the most annoying side of Brian Mulroney's personality. He projects a phoniness and sense of self-importance, sometimes coupled with pettiness.

As much as he can be charming and naturally engaging, Brian Mulroney also loves to be the centre of attention. I suppose that most, if not all, politicans do, to varying degrees. Jean Chretien, for instance, for all his "ordinary" ways, totally takes over any conversation he gets into. It's as though he doesn't feel he's performing if he doesn't have a funny story to tell, usually about himself.

Brian Mulroney prefers to be witty. When he tells stories, they are never lengthy ones, but he always tries to make you feel that they are thoughtful ones. The remaining part of his small talk is made up of one-liners, some of which he has used a hundred times—as somebody who sticks close to him will quickly find out. How many times did I hear the one about 24 Sussex being "public housing?" How many times did he say about his youngest son, that "Nicolas told me this" or "Nicolas told me that?" In the early days, when the Canadian public was still mesmerized by his wife's beauty and charm, he would use Mila's name instead.

If he likes to make people laugh, he seldom chuckles at other people's jokes and witticisms. I've often thought he doesn't even listen to them. The only funny stories he truly enjoys are those that depict people he knows in embarrassing situations—except his right honourable self, of course. He sometimes has his intimate friends or aides repeat those stories more than once, to get a good laugh out of them. The more they are embellished, the better.

One would think that being prime minister would be enough to impress anybody. But it seems Brian isn't satisfied until he's gone a little too far.

One of the pettiest things he did, while I was press secretary, I only heard about. I didn't spread it and pretended I never heard it, because I was sure my sources were telling the truth, and I was terrified of the story showing up in the media.

It happened, at least twice, at one of those dinner-parties at 24 Sussex, where the beautiful people of Canada, including some members of the Ottawa media—not me—were invited. As the story goes, Brian, while giving a guided tour of his estate to some of the wives of his guests, would casually show a second-floor room where, he said, "Margaret smoked pot." He was referring, of course, to Pierre Trudeau's former wife.

Well, anybody else could have gotten away with such harmless gossip, but it seemed to me it wasn't the kind of thing expected of a prime minister. And I couldn't understand how Mulroney, who was careful about every word he uttered in front of friend and foe alike, could sink to this wink-wink, nudge-nudge kind of scuttlebutt.

But, as much as he liked to impress people, I witnessed at least one occasion where he had to feel he failed miserably. It was in March, 1986, in Washington, immediately following our return visit to the White House.

The prime minister had agreed to do an editorial board at the prestigious *Washington Post*. It was quite a thrill for me to meet the legendary Ben Bradlee, publisher of the *Post*, and his team of top editors.

The editorial board was an "off-the-record" event. I didn't like those, and neither did Bill Fox, who was also present. First, because they were close to useless, since they generated often-obscure editorials, and no great headlines. But more importantly, because Mulroney tended to sound like a gossiper when he talked without the risk of being reported.

In any case, I can remember a strange look coming over his face when, all of a sudden, Ben Bradlee got up after about an hour, to say politely that he had already booked a previous engagement and would have to excuse himself. I thought he would never have done that to the president—and I'd bet a lot that the same painful thought went through The Boss's mind. No one dared raise it with him, though. He probably would have blamed it on us, anyway.

The man does think a lot of himself. Anybody who touches him should be thankful.

Which explains, I suppose, why he not only likes, but expects, to be served. Sooner or later, if you work closely enough to Brian Mulroney, you will fall victim to the get-me-a-coffee syndrome.

Most aides don't seem to mind serving him, though. It almost becomes a conditioned reflex. Like football players, trained to jump on loose balls to recover fumbles, The Boss's minions are taught to make sure his every need is met.

It's all part of what his praetorian guard used to call his "comfort zone." For him to perform at maximum efficiency, he must not be stressed by any other action, including getting his own cup of coffee.

Although I instinctively feel guilty whenever I'm being waited on, I didn't mind doing my share of the servile chores. Probably because I didn't have to do it very often. But I'm sure some of my journalistic colleagues must have had a chuckle when, during an official interview, for instance, The Boss would turn to his press secretary and say, "Michel, could you get me a coffee?"

And Michel would dutifully get up and fetch. If it made him feel good about himself and the interview, I didn't mind looking like his lapdog. I came to think of it as part of the job definition.

On one occasion, though, he took me completely by surprise. We were in his office on the third floor of Parliament's Centre Block. There was another staffer there. I can't remember who it was, but he must have been higher ranking than me, because I was the one The Boss picked as his servant that day.

All of a sudden, in the middle of a conversation about

government matters, he turned to me and said, "Michel, could you get me a glass of water?"

I was so stunned, I wasn't sure I'd heard right. He wasn't asking me to go get water somewhere else in the building. He wanted me to walk about twelve feet to the pitcher on the corner of his coffee table, and pour him a glass of iced water. Of course, he could have walked the same distance himself and kept on talking all the while. But his reflex was to order somebody to do it, and I was the lowest-ranking officer around.

When he saw the look on my face, I felt, for one of the rare times, that he was perhaps a little embarrassed, and that the words had escaped his mouth without thinking. It was an awkward moment and, to avoid making it worse, I got the water.

He never asked me again.

When I got back to my office, though, I was still flabbergasted as I told the story to one of the more mature secretaries. In a motherly way, she said, "You're not used to being served, are you? That's good."

The eagerness of people in his entourage to please him has a lot to do with what Mulroney imposes on himself. From morning to night, he never stops. He is always "on." His day starts around 6:00 a.m., and never ends before the latest evening news is over.

Mulroney is totally consumed by his work. The only other thing that matters to him is his family. But since, so far, they seem to be growing up beautifully and without trouble, he concentrates most of his time on his other passion. What else would he do? He doesn't drink, doesn't smoke, doesn't have a hobby and doesn't practise any sport. A man has to find a way to pass the time and get his rocks off, I suppose. He does that with politics.

When he goes on holidays, he's supposed to get away from it all. But everybody in his entourage knows that it is only a matter of time before the phone rings, and the familiar voice asks how things are back in the capital.

When he's by himself like that, he often takes the opportunity to write a thoughtful speech, which he will deliver to his staff, cabinet or the caucus, on his return.

His vision of government and the country, usually. He wants it to be more emotional than the others but, in fact, he finds it hard to convey real feelings, which I've always believed hampers his ability to sound sincere when he speaks publicly. Just as he finds it extremely difficult to laugh at himself and apologize for his mistakes.

He has learned that self-deprecation is a must to survive in politics, but he does it because he has to. He still doesn't understand what's so funny about his perfect person.

As for apologizing for his mistakes, I remember the first time he did it as prime minister. It was after the first Wilson budget, when Canada's seniors revolted against the government that threatened to de-index their pensions. I don't know how many times I heard him say then, in private, that there was nothing wrong with saying you're sorry. He sounded more like he was trying to convince himself than his listener.

The telephone is not the only essential instrument that is never far from Brian Mulroney. Being his executive assistant, as only three people have been to date, is a lot like being the curator of Mulroney paraphernalia. The big briefcase carries all the essentials to make sure The Boss looks good, feels good and smells good.

Smell, you say? Well, yeah. Let me tell you the story about the mouth spray.

I was at the National Press Club for a lunch I intended to turn into a long one. Rick Morgan called to say The Boss wanted to see me before Question Period. I wasn't expecting to meet him that day, since nothing major was going on, so I'd had a couple of beers with my journalistic buddies.

I rushed back to the Hill, and didn't have time to pick up mints to cover the smell of booze. When I got to the prime minister's office, I frantically asked my friend Rick to pass me one of The Boss's Listerine mouth sprays, explaining my problem.

As he did when Mulroney asked him, he reached in his pocket and handed me the Listerine.

I barely had time to *pssst-pssst* my mouth before the door of his office swung open. We were both standing right there. Quickly, I shoved the spray in my coat pocket and tried to look perfectly nonchalant.

Mulroney said "Hi," then turned to Rick, put his hand to his mouth, and mimicked spraying it. Oh, my God! He wanted his mouth spray!

Calmly, while I was dying inside, Rick reached for another container in his pocket.

*Pheeeew!* I thought I was home free, thanks to Morgan's total preparedness. But when Mulroney tried the spray, it didn't work. Mechanically, he simply extended his hand, asking for another one.

My heart sank. Slowly, Rick Morgan turned his head, to look at me with a dumb smile on his face, and extended his own hand. And I, looking every bit like the kid who gets caught with his dad's cigarettes, just as slowly took the mouth spray out of my own pocket and handed it to a shocked prime minister.

Mulroney stared at the Listerine spray, stared at me, stared at Rick, two or three times, without saying a word, a disbelieving look on his face. Suddenly, he knew how the Three Bears, of Goldilocks fame, felt. *Who's been messing with my mouth spray?*

After a few seconds of this, which seemed like hours, he finally entered the washroom, shaking his head. Morgan would say afterwards—whenever some kooky thing would happen, and we were involved—that the PM thought we were playing "headgames" with him.

But, as demanding as he may have been with his staff, Mulroney was also a very tolerant man, when it came to human weakness and less-than-professional behaviour. He knew, for instance, that at any point in time, many members of his staff were dating each other. He never liked it and never thought it was very smart, but he would not complain or call people on the carpet for it.

I remember one time, when Mila was having a conversation with me on the Challenger about how I should get a steady girlfriend. She had seen me with Ann Charron at a recent wedding, and commented that she was "cute," and that I should be serious about her. She didn't seem to know that Ann was working for me, or that we had been seeing each other for over a year at the time.

All this time, The Boss was absorbed in his briefing books, and I thought he wasn't listening. But when Mila said that, without looking away from his papers, he said, "She works for us."

"What?" said Mila.

"She works for us"

He never said another word. She just gave me a disapproving look and shook her head.

Yes, they were both very patient with me. The following story perhaps gives an idea of the kind of reasonable and kind man Brian Mulroney can be.

It had all started at Mama Teresa's restaurant, Ottawa's most famous political hang-out. I was having dinner with a female friend, when who walked in but Peter Pocklington, the millionaire owner of the Edmonton Oilers hockey club. It was in the fall of 1986, and Mila had just spent months organizing an exhibition game between the Oilers and the Stanley Cup champions Montreal Canadiens, at Ottawa's Civic Centre.

I'm a Canadiens fan. Pocklington was in the company of his general manager, Glen Sather. I went over to their table and introduced myself. They didn't seem too impressed, but I really got their attention when I said that the Canadiens would win the game the following night.

"You wanta bet?" said the millionaire.

"Sure! How much?" I said.

"One thousand?" Peter Puck blurted out.

I don't know if it showed, but I swallowed heavily at that moment. One grand was to him like ten dollars to me. With Italian wine boosting my courage, my stupid street bravado took over, as I shot back, "All right. One thousand." We shook hands.

I went back to my table and my lady friend. She was impressed, but I said under my breath, "I must be out of my mind."

The Canadiens lost. I didn't pay up that night, since

I didn't see Pocklington and didn't go looking for him, either. But a gambling debt is a debt of honour, and I had every intention of settling it as soon as I saw the man again.

It happened a few months later in Quebec City, where the prime minister was attending the annual NHL all-star game that, for the first time, pitted the year's best players against the Soviet national hockey team. Mulroney attended a pre-game cocktail party, and Pocklington was there, along with Sather.

I took my chequebook out of my breast pocket, walked over to him and said, "Mr Pocklington, I believe I owe you some money."

He was totally baffled and seemed to think it was some kind of joke, when I handed him the $1,000.

"What's this?" he said.

I tried to refresh his memory, but it was Sather who said, "I remember that bet!"

Pocklington thanked me, and slipped it into his pocket like it was nothing. It looked like it meant so little to him, I felt like crying.

Still, I walked away feeling that I had done what I had to do. There would be other bets.

Later on in the night, after the hockey game, I was up in my hotel room when Mila's assistant, Bonnie Brownlee, walked in.

"The Boss wants to see you," she said.

I could tell by the look on her face that something out of the ordinary was going on. What had I been caught at this time?

I went over to his suite. Mulroney was sitting at a desk with his shirt sleeves rolled up and his reading glasses on. He appeared to be working on a speech. When I walked in, he didn't even salute me. He just looked up slightly and, with a stern face, handed me a piece of green paper. It was my cheque to Pocklington.

Stunned, I stared at the cheque, not knowing what to think or say. I finally stuttered, "Uh...it was a bet..."

"You don't have the kind of money to make bets like that," replied the prime minister.

"You're right, I don't," I said. "Thank you."

I learned later, through Bonnie, that Pocklington had given it to Mila for her to donate, if she wished, to her chosen charity. When she saw the signature on the cheque, however, she knew I couldn't afford it. She was well aware of the monthly support payments I had to make for my three daughters. She was already collecting millions annually for cystic fibrosis. She couldn't accept it and, when she showed it to her husband, neither could he.

They didn't have to do that. Other people would have said, rightly, "Tough luck for the idiot!" The Mulroneys are not like that. Few people in the outside world know that. But those who were phoned or visited in the hospital, or given moral support when their lives turned sour, do. I know of a few national reporters who were touched by Mulroney that way, but don't boast about it too loudly.

There are those who will say, cynically, that The Boss is merely playing politician, and that he is exploiting the situation to make people indebted to him. There is undoubtedly that temptation in every political person, and he is no exception. But, believe it or not, Mulroney is wary of such behaviour. He's not blind or deaf to the criticism that is levelled his way about how phony and devious he is. Consequently, he constantly second-guesses himself, when his aides suggest that he take advantage of certain situations to score a few political points.

Take Canadian sprinter Ben Johnson's ill-fated Olympic victory in Seoul, Korea. Remember how the prime minister phoned from Ottawa to congratulate a steroid-boosted Johnson, moments after the great event and hours before the disaster that followed?

I was surprised when I saw Mulroney do that on TV. He had always refused to jump on such bandwagons, when I was working for him. He thought it smacked of political opportunism.

In fact, as I learned later, it wasn't his idea at all.

"It was all my fault," then-sports-minister Jean Charest admitted to me, long after the incident. "He didn't want to do it, but I'm the one who convinced him that Canadians were expecting him to do so."

As Mulroney's luck would have it, the one time when he didn't listen to his own best advice, it blew up in his face, and columnists, like myself, took a mean pleasure in exposing him. When the next cabinet shuffle came, Jean Charest, one of the most promising young ministers, didn't get a promotion and was stuck with the steroids mess and a minor portfolio. I could just imagine The Boss saying, "So you wanted me to phone Ben Johnson, eh...?"

All this is to say that Mulroney's negative image is sometimes built on things he has little to do with. The net result, though, is that his sincerity is constantly being questioned, even when he deals with more serious matters than a juiced-up Olympic sprinter.

Take his stand against the apartheid regime in South Africa. As much as he put time, effort and action into it, at home it was largely perceived as a purely opportunistic stand that had little to do with Mulroney's personal convictions and principles. Well, let me tell you a story about that, and judge for yourself.

The prime minister was attending a huge Tory fundraising dinner in Toronto. Minutes before he was to leave his hotel suite to go down to the event at the Convention Centre, there was a major commotion on his floor.

People started running up and down the hall, panic-stricken. I heard something about External Affairs Minister Joe Clark being summoned up urgently to the prime minister's suite.

The Boss was refusing to go down to the dinner, because he had found out that some brilliant Tory had invited none other than South African ambassador Glen Babb to the event.

Mulroney was livid. To make things worse, the man was to be seated at a neighbouring table, and had been invited by a member of the PC Canada Fund's board of directors.

The prime minister was adamant. "Either he goes, or I don't show up!"

Babb and his entire table left. The media present for the event, amazingly, never saw it happen, nor heard about it. I was tempted to leak it, thinking it would perhaps show Mulroney's sincerity in his anti-apartheid battle. But I decided not to. What would have been seen as a glorious gesture for anybody else, always seemed to backfire when it came to him. To this day, I have kept it to myself.

Historians will judge Brian Mulroney a lot more kindly than his contemporaries. They will be able to analyze the success of his policies without their vision being blurred by the distrustful public image of the calculating politician.

Mulroney will likely be seen as a prime minister who had a more pragmatic vision of Canada's role in the world, and gave the country tools it didn't have before to succeed on the international scene.

In his short time in office, Mulroney has successfully worked to make Canada a member of the G-7, giving it a real voice among the seven countries that run the finances of the planet. Against all odds, he has settled an unending squabble with Quebec and played a key role in creating the Francophonie, the French equivalent of the Commonwealth. He also got Canada a seat on the United Nations Security Council, and has continued to be effective at Commonwealth meetings. As a result, Canada is the only country on Earth that enjoys such a privileged position on so many key international bodies.

Mulroney's concern had a little to do with prestige—including his own—but was fundamentally economic, just as it was with free trade, and even the Meech Lake Accord. When Meech ran into trouble in the spring of 1990, one of his main concerns was that, on the international scene—in Europe and Japan in particular—leaders were not taking Canada seriously anymore.

But for all his accomplishments, he will always be full of blarney. He can't help it.

**Chapter 15**

"How are things between you and Mulroney now?"

"He doesn't talk to me"

"If you asked him for an interview, would he grant it to you?"

"No...I'd be lying if I said otherwise."

"I thank you for your frankness."

That's it, I thought. Another one bites the dust. I figured I had just kissed goodbye to a national columnist's job at *The Toronto Sun*.

Some other time, perhaps. I already thought it was a miracle that I had even gotten this far, to publisher Paul Godfrey's office. Be serious! How could a franco from Vanier, and former political flack, delude himself into thinking the *Sun* would ever seriously consider hiring him? After all, this was the paper that had lynched me publicly, two years earlier.

Those thoughts were going through my mind, as I heard Godfrey say, "We would like to have you on our team."

The scene was unreal, in slow-motion, as when your

senses react to some sudden event like a car accident.

Even if they were to offer me the job, I never expected it would happen so quickly. I had come down to Toronto at Bob Fife's urging to meet with executive editor Les Pyette. Joe O'Donnell, the *Sun*'s Ottawa columnist, had accepted a prestigious posting to the chain's newly opened Washington bureau, and they were looking for a replacement.

Before we went up to Godfrey's office with editor John Downing and Fife, Pyette had told me that he had other candidates, but that I was his preferred choice. But I still had to "go to the sixth floor" and meet Godfrey, before any decision was to be made.

When I came out of that meeting, I felt groggy. It was too much, too soon. I had started writing columns in English on a regular basis only six months earlier. Until then, almost all my journalistic work had been done in French. The incredible events of the previous two years flashed before my eyes, as I celebrated with Fife, Downing and Pyette that night in Toronto; the fall from grace in the PMO, the stressful writing of the book, Mulroney's rage, the *Le Droit* strike, the election campaign. It all came back in one unbelievable film. It was stranger than fiction.

But I was there, at the *Sun*, with 600,000 readers across the country.

The newly created *Ottawa Sun* headed my first column: "Yoo Hoo, Brian, Guess Who?" They also ran an ad that read: "So, What's Michel Saying?" a pun on the title of my first account of life with Brian.

For the very first time, I felt like I had truly turned the corner. The *Sun* made me start to feel like a journalist again. And, in a liberating way, I started to see Mulroney more clearly, with a strange sense of serenity.

I didn't care that he was angry at me anymore. For the first time, I felt it was his problem, not mine.

That's why I really enjoyed one of my first assignments.

We went back to Baie Comeau.

There wasn't much to the trip, but Bob Fife thought it

was a natural for a colour story and a columnist. And who better to do it than Brian's number-one pain in the ass?

We were treated to one of Mulroney's patented phony numbers. He went to visit the Quebec and Ontario Paper Co.—which the locals still call the Quebec Northshore—where his father worked all his life as an electrician. That's also where Brian claims he once "was a truck driver." Of course, he hasn't driven too many vehicles over the past ten years or so. The Iron Ore chauffeurs, provided to the president of the company, and the prime-ministerial RCMP bodyguards have taken care of that chore.

It's lunchtime at the plant, and the workers are headed to the cafeteria with their lunchboxes. Brian's handlers have turned this into the day's photo opportunity: the prime minister eating with the common folk.

His cufflinks shining and his dark suit impeccable, he extends his hand over the fries with gravy and the overcooked cafeteria roast beef. Just one of the boys. Maybe a little bit overdressed, but in his mind, the people expect a prime minister to look like a prime minister—especially in his hometown.

They still call him by his first name, though, and, digging into that phenomenal memory of his, he manages to remember each and every one of them. The old school of politics.

There is only one problem: Brian is expected to eat, and he never does that before the cameras. God knows what could happen! Soup dripping down his chin, a front-page picture with his mouth wide-open or his cheeks distorted by a lump of food. Not his idea of the perfect candidate.

He orders a soup and coffee. Intrigued, I wait to see if he's actually going to eat it. I'm standing on the camera riser, because I know that, with their zoom lenses, the TV guys can get a better look at what's going on.

Mulroney, trying to look casual while chatting with the workers, picks up his spoon, dips it in the soup bowl, and dangerously brings it toward his mouth. A TV cameraman starts chuckling. "There's no soup in the spoon," he says, incredulously. Mulroney's faking it.

It reminds a veteran technician of how former Social Credit leader Fabien Roy once got terribly embarrassed because he had dared put something in his mouth in front of the cameras.

It was during the 1980 election campaign, when Social Credit finally got wiped off the political map. Fabien Roy was visiting, of all places, a slaughterhouse where they made sausage.

It was a messy affair from beginning to finish, with blood and guts on public display. At some point during the gory visit, one of the plant's managers handed over a raw wiener to their famous guest.

Roy felt he had to accept it as a priceless gift, especially with the cameras rolling. He took a bite, but he didn't have the heart to swallow it. In fact, for a minute, the media people present thought he was going to throw up.

But no. Fabien simply kept the piece of wiener in his mouth during the half-hour visit to the slaughterhouse, not being able to gulp it down or spit it out. Through it all, an amused press contingent could see the Social Credit leader playing with the piece of wiener, sometimes shifting it to the left cheek, sometimes to the right, and then making it almost disappear under his tongue.

Maybe Brian had the right idea after all.

But his aides weren't always as careful as he was, as they demonstrated a few weeks later. That was when the Madame Tussaud incident happened.

The story really begins before the 1988 election campaign. Mulroney's office then had a standing invitation from the famous London wax museum to turn Brian into the dummy he had every right to be.

A few months before the election, while looking for some clever ways to make The Boss look good, some of the prime minister's brilliant handlers thought it would be a great coup to get their man turned to wax. But Madame Tussaud could read polls, too. As much as she had wanted Our Boy Brian earlier on, she was now kind of lukewarm on the idea.

So it sort of died, until Mulroney pulled off the unexpected and won a second majority. The fickle Madame was begging for Brian's love again.

Recently appointed chief-of-staff Stanley Hartt was handling the request. He thought it was a great idea, consulted with a few of the PM's advisers, and decided Brian was destined, indeed, to be a dummy.

He only forgot one minor detail. He didn't bother telling Mulroney about it.

The Boss found out in the papers that his estranged Madame was planning a reconciliation on March 12, 1989, while he would be in London for a visit with Margaret Thatcher. Predictably, he hit the roof.

How could they set him up for such a clownish event, without even consulting with him in the first place? Didn't they know that the media were only waiting for such opportunities to make him look like a leader totally full of himself?

He kicked and screamed, and told his staff to cancel the event.

Instead, they stalled. It was almost impossible to get out of it, now that Madame Tussaud had announced it. Maybe he would change his mind before the trip, which would take him to an environmental conference in The Hague, and to London.

That's where I came in. The *Sun* sent me to cover the overseas trip. I was looking forward to it. No matter how insignificant it was, something weird and entertaining always seemed to happen on Mulroney's international outings. This one would not be different.

A relatively small press contingent filled the back of the Armed Forces Boeing 707, as the flight took off for the Netherlands for a seminar that was assuredly important, but not too "news-sexy."

On the way over, as rookie press secretary Gilbert Lavoie strolled over to the back of the aircraft, to mix with the ruffians he had been one of a few weeks earlier, I asked him about the wax museum.

"Is the Madame Tussaud thing on or not?" I asked, innocently.

He didn't give a direct answer, and appeared rather embarrassed by the subject. I learned later that Gilbert, on his maiden voyage and still inexperienced in the science of Mulroney-handling, had made the mistake of raising the matter several times with the prime minister. All he had gotten for an answer was a dirty look and a cold shoulder.

I knew The Boss better than he did, and I sensed in Lavoie's silence that something was wrong. I guessed right: Brian was playing hard to get.

For his staff, this was the ultimate nightmare. They were stuck with a commitment to an event Mulroney wanted no part of. To make things worse, the media were watching their every move, chuckling all the time at Brian's reluctance to be turned to wax.

I wrote a column out of The Hague on how he planned to stand up the world-famous Madame. That only made the prime minister's temperature rise a little more—especially coming from me.

The crunch came on the short flight from The Hague to London. Pressured by a pesky media corps, which was enjoying every minute of this embarrassing episode, Gilbert Lavoie once again gathered up his courage and walked over to Mulroney.

The Boss was standing in the aisle, leaning casually on the back of a seat, and having a relaxed conversation with some of his aides. Lavoie changed the mood of the moment when he said, "Mr. Prime Minister, the Madame Tussaud museum, the boys want to know what you are going to do..."

After holding back for all those weeks, Mulroney finally let it go, as he stared at Gilbert and said, "Madame Tussaud? I need that as much as I need a hole in the head."

He then turned on his heel and slammed the door of his front cabin shut. His staff was no further ahead, and his press secretary had just experienced his first Mulroney put-down.

When they got to London, Madame Tussaud was

forced to cancel the posing and measuring session she had planned for Brian, and the elaborate tour she had organized for the Canadian media. He didn't go to her...but she went to him. Against his will, Mulroney's handlers managed to drag him, still kicking and screaming, to a suite in his hotel, where the Tussaud waxers sized him up. After about two hours and what seemed like a thousand snapshots, the prime minister was set free of his tormentors.

Later that year, though, he had to relive those painful moments at the annual National Press Gallery Dinner. In the the show that followed the dinner—a musical parody of the year's main political events, put on by the members of the Gallery—the actor impersonating Mulroney was brought on stage on a rolling platform, and made to look like a wax statue.

When his advisor Luc Lavoie (not Gilbert) came back from an advance trip to Europe, months after the incident, Mulroney asked him, "So, how was London?"

"I went to see your statue," Lavoie replied to an unsuspecting prime minister. This time, he burst out laughing.

But back to the Hague-London trip. Something quite extraordinary happened to me then.

Luc Lavoie and I had discussed privately the fact that Mulroney wouldn't even acknowledge my presence. I said I understood his attitude, and that he probably wouldn't answer my questions, if I were to ask any in a scrum or press conference.

"I'm not sure you're right about that," said Lavoie.

Was it a cue from Mulroney? Did that mean the feud was over?

I didn't know. But there was a press conference scheduled in The Hague where I, like all other Canadian journalists, could ask questions more easily than in a messy scrum.

I decided to take the big leap. I would never have admitted it to my colleagues then, but I was terrified at the thought of facing Mulroney. Nobody likes to be made a fool of in public. I'm no exception.

I got one of the first questions. Trying to forget who I was speaking to, I asked the prime minister about the *Satanic Verses* affair, and the fact that British author Salman Rushdie had been sentenced to death by Iran's Ayatollah Khomeini. The story had been in the news for some time, but it would be the first time Mulroney would set foot in Britain since it had begun.

Mulroney's powerful jaw toughened, as he clenched his teeth and gave me one of the coldest stares I have ever felt. But he answered. And the answer he gave was probably the best of the press conference, possibly the whole trip.

When it was over, I felt like an enormous weight had been lifted from my shoulders. And, from what he said to his aides after the press conference, I think Mulroney felt the same way. He confided to them that it was "his duty" to answer my questions. And he added, "Besides, Michel is polite."

The next day, he gave an organized scrum in front of 10 Downing Street, after his meeting with Margaret Thatcher. Since I had asked him the day before about whether he intended to discuss the Rushdie case with the Iron Lady, I felt obligated to inquire about what had been said.

But this was not as easy as a disciplined press conference. Almost every reporter present was trying to get his attention, and screaming questions at the same time. I didn't even open my mouth and just raised one little finger, when Mulroney shut everybody up by pointing at me and saying, "Oui, Michel?"

I mumbled my question in French. As soon as he was finished, the media pack started yapping again. I tried to follow up with another question, but couldn't be heard. What did Mulroney do? He silenced them again and pointed to me. "Michel?"

He was killing me with kindness. I felt like an idiot when I stuttered, "Could you repeat your answer in English, please?"

He did.

Later, when someone asked radio reporter Graham

Jardine, who was also on the trip, whether it was true that Mulroney had spoken to me, he summed it up this way. "It got so bad, it was disgusting! Michel here, Michel there!"

On the flight back to Canada, Mulroney came to the back of the plane to shoot the breeze with the reporters. It was the first time he had done so when I was part of the travelling media.

He stopped to ask me how I liked the trip. I said I could never get used to jetlag.

"Neither can I. You never get used to it," he said.

I had been rehabilitated.

It would make my job a little easier, knowing that Mulroney had finally, grudgingly, accepted that I had indeed returned to the other side.

I had no doubt that he was still deeply annoyed by my knowledge of the inside operation of the government, and his office in particular. I did possess a lot of embarrassing and revealing information.

But it wasn't until I started work on this book that, while going through the personal things and papers I had left over from my PMO days, I stumbled on an old document I didn't know I had.

It was marked "Secret" and was signed by Clerk of the Privy Council Paul Tellier, on June 2, 1986. It referred to something called the "Business Transfer Tax." Tellier had handwritten "PM—Important" and signed at the top of the "Memorandum for the Prime Minister."

If you've never heard about this tax, that's because its name changed to "Goods and Services Tax," or GST, when the time came to sell it to a skeptical public.

The Tories had announced their intention of setting up such a tax before the 1988 election campaign. But what could have become a difficult political matter for them was totally forgotten, when the sole issue of the campaign became the Canada-U.S. free trade agreement.

Once that was out of the way, though, the GST quickly became the most controversial and unpopular government measure brought down by the Mulroney regime.

So the document I had, in hindsight, made rather

interesting reading. It showed where the crucial decisions were made on the GST—and how close Canadians came to being spared it.

Don't ask me why I kept this one. It was purely a fluke. I had been very careful not to take any sensitive government documents with me when I left. This one must have ended up at the bottom of the box.

The letter, from June 1986, to the prime minister, reads: "Mr. (Michael) Wilson urgently wishes to discuss the BTT with you next week, at the same time as he discusses the proposed June Economic and Fiscal Statement. Mr. Wilson wants your agreement and full support to proceed with the BTT..."

Tellier goes on: "He (Wilson) will stress that the BTT is crucial to the Government's _ever_ having any fiscal flexibility. In this mandate, that flexibility would be reflected in the removal of the income-tax surtaxes, probably in the February 1988 budget. A greater degree of fiscal flexibility would be available in the first mandate." (_ever_ is underlined in the original.)

What Tellier, quoting Wilson, was suggesting was that the government had no manoeuvring room to introduce any new programmes or reduce taxes in an election year, if the BTT didn't become a reality.

Tellier states that "provincial acquiescence would be important in this regard," but does not say that it is essential, which probably explains why the discussions with the provinces on the sales tax eventually broke up.

One thing that is important, though, is the GST's link to free trade. Tellier writes: "Sales tax reform is strongly linked to the Canada-U.S. trade thrust, in Mr. Wilson's view, as it would encourage exports, remove the pro-import bias in the present sales tax, and allow Canada to respond to U.S. tax reform initiatives which may result in lower marginal tax rates in the U.S."

The Tories certainly never told us that during the free trade debate. Linking two such controversial issues would have undoubtedly produced disastrous electoral results. Can you imagine telling Canadians, "We need more taxes if we get free trade?" Yet, Tellier, officially the most reliable mandarin in the Public Service, claims Michael Wilson thought the GST was essential to Canada being in a competitive position with the American markets.

Tellier follows that up with a crucial point: "Most fundamentally, the BTT is the only potential source of new revenues which the Department of Finance has been able to identify. The ultimate resolution of the federal government's fiscal problem will depend in substantial part on implementation of the BTT." In other words, it's the only way they can raise taxes and possibly get the deficit under control.

That of course, doesn't jibe at all with what Michael Wilson was struggling to say early on in the GST debate, that it wouldn't be used to reduce the deficit. It is also clear that, rather than "replacing a bad tax," as the Tories have been saying about the GST replacing the "unfair" manufacturer's tax, it is, in fact, a tax increase. It is also flexible enough to permit further tax increases in the future, something the government has never ruled out.

Tellier reminds the prime minister that he is facing some tough opposition to the new tax within his own cabinet's powerful Priorities and Planning Committee: "As you are also aware, a number of P & P Ministers have expressed reservations about proceeding with the BTT at this time. These include concerns about the following issues:

-the tight timetable for implementation;

-the 4,000 - 5,000 additional staff who will be required by Revenue Canada to administer the BTT;

-the possible reaction of the nearly 2 million businesses which will be brought within the federal sales tax system for the first time;

-the apparent absence of major fiscal benefits to the Government (although Mr. Wilson is currently placing much more emphasis on the fiscal benefits of the BTT than he did in his initial presentations to P & P)."

The PCO Clerk adds: "If you agree with Mr. Wilson that the BTT should proceed at this time, I would recommend that you and Mr. Wilson try to secure the active support of two or three other senior Ministers (including Mr. MacKay) for this course of action, before you call the Government's decision... Successful implementation of the BTT will require determination and steadfastness on the part of the entire Ministry and a solid core of commitment among senior ministers is absolutely crucial to success." Elmer MacKay was then minister of revenue.

Paul Tellier ends on this ominous note: "The meeting with Mr. Wilson is urgently required next week, because Stanley Hartt is convinced that failure to reach a decision on the BTT by the end of June would close off the Government's options. In other words, taking no explicit decision before the end of June would amount to an implicit decision on the part of the Government not to introduce the BTT during this mandate." (*explicit* and *implicit* are underlined in the original.)

Michael Wilson committed the government to the BTT and fiscal reform on July 18, 1986, six weeks after this memo reached the prime minister's desk.

Stanley Hartt was then deputy minister of finance. He left that position before the end of the mandate, but came back after the 1988 election as chief-of-staff to the prime minister. With his assistant, Tom Trbovich, formerly Michael Wilson's chief-of-staff, Hartt headed the GST offensive from an even more powerful position, the PMO. Once such a strong supporter of the tax, from the beginning, got so close to Mulroney, the GST became almost irreversible.

Three years later, in 1989, as I was observing from the journalistic sidelines, we were definitely stuck with the GST and Michael Wilson, Mulroney's only minister of finance to date.

Few anticipated, though, as the tough budget of the new mandate loomed menacingly on the political horizon, that the phlegmatic Wilson was on the verge of a catastrophe.

And it had a name: Doug Small.

**Chapter 16**

Doug Small wondered what it was all about.

The bigwigs at Global TV wanted him to fly down to Toronto urgently. It was a fateful day he would never forget. In his worst nightmares, he couldn't have expected what was waiting for him at the other end. Neither could most of the people who knew him.

The silver-haired Small, with the perennial smile and the easy-going outlook on life, showed up at the offices of Global TV a little anxious, but not overly concerned.

He should have been. This was an ambush.

The first words he heard were, "We think you're an alcoholic."

Small's heart sank to the bottom of his gut.

The accusation did not come lightly. Small's accusers produced a scrapbook of pictures, to prove their claim. Most of the snapshots were of the 1988 election campaign, and depicted their Ottawa Bureau chief in various embarrassing poses on the leaders' planes.

Some of the pictures, in fact, had already appeared in newspapers around the country—one of them had Small wearing a Mulroney look-alike mask, and being pounded on the head with a foam bat by the wife of John Turner, Geills. Another unpublished picture had him sleeping in his airplane seat, handcuffed to the flight attendants' booze tray.

Now, in the good old days of journalism, people would have scoffed at such evidence. Of course reporters drank! Wasn't that part of being one?

But this was the Age of the New Morality, where more and more conscientious members of the trade were switching to Perrier. And besides, Small was on TV, where even the newsroom is a soap opera with perfect-looking, perfect-talking, just simply perfect people.

Once his bosses dropped the bomb in Doug's lap, they had him taken to an abuse treatment centre, Bellwood, where a counsellor was waiting to make an evaluation of his condition.

When Doug Small got back on the plane to Ottawa that day, he was a totally destroyed man.

"I had no self-respect left," he says today. "Nothing."

He didn't have a drink on the flight. He couldn't get himself to bring it to his lips.

He then spent what he calls "the worst weekend of my life." News of Small's demise had quickly spread through the press gallery fishbowl, and friends were trying to rally to his side.

They were trying to help, but they didn't. They simply worsened his condition. The most ironic part of it was that some of those who phoned were evidently pissed to the eyeballs themselves, telling him he didn't have a problem, and suggesting that he should sue his employers.

Small can laugh about it today, but he sure wasn't doing any laughing then. On the Saturday before his admission to the treatment centre, he did something rather strange; he got a haircut. He wanted to look good for it.

I suppose he didn't suspect that he was about to room with a bunch of drug and alcohol abusers, who looked like anything but TV anchormen.

"It was scary stuff," he says, of the moment he walked into the place and was confronted with the people he was now being identified with.

It took him a few days to get over the shame. And it took him a little longer to accept that he had a problem, but Doug Small now claims that he was "lucky." He was lucky that the people at Global cared enough to give him the chance to clean up his act.

Mind you, there are still a lot of people on the Hill who think he never had a problem, but he's happy about being clean and sober.

"There are days when you just feel like the shitters, don't kid yourself," he told me about his abstinence. "But then there are days when you feel great about yourself."

The reason I tell this story is that it may be important to the reader to know what hell Doug Small had gone through in the weeks leading up to April 26, 1989.

On that night, I had already been home for a few hours when the phone rang. It was my bureau chief, Bob Fife.

"You've got to come back in," he said.

He sounded very excited.

"What?" I said.

"You've got to come back in. The budget has been leaked! Wilson might have to resign!"

"Fuck you! Budgets don't get leaked...it must be some kind of speculation again."

"No. I tell you, Small was on Global, waving a copy of the budget-in-brief."

"He had a copy?"

"Yes," he said, impatiently.

"He didn't!"

"Don't you think this is important?" said Fife, disbelievingly.

This was getting out of hand. There I was, arguing about something I knew nothing about, simply because it was screwing up my day.

Finally, I suffered a massive attack of sanity, and relented. "He actually showed a document on TV?" I asked.

He had. Fife was right: this was big.

It's one thing for a reporter to have gotten privileged information from an anonymous source. It is quite another to actually get your hands on a budget document, and believe so much in its authenticity that you are prepared to put your journalistic credibility on the line and show it to the world.

In fact, this had never happened at the Canadian government level—except to Trudeau minister Marc Lalonde, who had accidentally let a TV cameraman film one incriminating page of his budget speech, using a zoom lens. And there was, of course, the timeless British parliamentary "budget tradition," where secrecy prior to publication was so important that a finance minister who could not ensure it was expected to resign.

The custom is not just the figment of somebody's vivid imagination. It is based on the assumption that certain greedy souls out there could profit financially from advance knowledge of its contents. That is why it is never made public, on budget day, before the stock market closes.

Now, I, for one, have long suspected that certain people with the right connections could easily find out inside information if they really wanted to, without necessarily being compromised by the possession of a document. The process and bureaucracy involved has simply become too big, and I believe that, although the minister of finance should do everything possible to protect budget secrecy, he cannot be asked to do the impossible.

As it turned out, it appeared that the copies of the budget-in-brief documents that came out ahead of time (we know now of at least two such copies) were smuggled out in a very innocuous way. What I mean is that you didn't have the deputy minister of finance phoning his broker to give him information. Blue-collar workers did the job.

Nevertheless, Mulroney's opposition didn't think so and, predictably, John Turner and Ed Broadbent asked for Michael Wilson's head.

All this was brought on by a drive to a Sunoco gas

station, by a reporter who was still asking himself some serious questions about his career future. Doug Small found it practical to meet there with the secret informer who had earlier phoned Global TV, because the service station was close to his home.

But it's interesting to note that the budget leak that almost brought down Michael Wilson, and caused seemingly endless aggravation to the Mulroney government, came very close to never happening at all.

Global TV first got a call from an anonymous informant, who told them he had a document that explained the budget—if they cared to know what was in it. The news reporter at the other end took down the information and verified its authenticity with the Ottawa Bureau.

Given all the speculation of the previous weeks, and the hints given by Michael Wilson himself, the information sounded good.

Global, however, didn't push to see the document. They merely ran an evening-news speculative piece about what was thought to be in Wilson's budget.

What happened next is straight out of a film script. The mysterious caller, who had watched the news to appreciate his sabotage, realized his intervention had not been taken as seriously as it should have been.

He then did the improbable thing. He phoned back.

He said that, if they weren't satisfied he was telling the truth, he had a document he was willing to give to them.

That was when Small came into the picture. His journalistic instincts, after years in the business, told him that, even if there was only a strong possibility this might not be a hoax, it was still better to check it out.

He drove to the Sunoco and waited in his car, as somebody he later called "a nondescript man" walked up to the car and said, "I think I have something you want."

He then handed over the copy of the budget-in-brief document.

A war veteran by the name of John Appleby was the man who walked over to Small's car on the night of April

26, and sent the Mulroney government into a tailspin. He was charged for it but, as this book goes to print, would not be convicted. Appleby certainly didn't know what he was getting himself into when he walked over to Doug Small's car, that night.

As the news of the leak spread like wildfire, pandemonium hit the Hill. Reporters who had been enjoying one leisurely evening, on the eve of what promised to be another tedious exercise of budget lock-up and of writing endless copy, suddenly found themselves in a mad dash for the deadline.

A lot of the "boys" had already spent a few too many hours at the National Press Club, and were very much enjoying themselves when the order to sober up came down like an angry wife walking in—okay, an angry spouse. It must be said that the leak happened a couple of days before the annual Press Gallery bash, and that quite a few reporters—some from out of town—were getting a deserved coat of primer before the event. Everybody was now expecting a tabling of the budget that same evening, to beat the opening of the stock markets.

The reaction was just as frenzied among members of the Opposition.

John Turner, thirsting for blood, told his aides, "We've got the sons-of-bitches on the run!"

Or so they thought.

Ministerial limousines rushed to the Langevin Block—and parked on the wide sidewalk, as usual. Never had so many of them been seen bunched in together on the corner of Elgin and Wellington, across from Ottawa's War Memorial.

On the other side of the street, the opposition members and government backbenchers were being unloaded from the Commons' little green buses, for an unscheduled sitting. Some still had wine left in the bottle, as they quickly exited the Parliamentary restaurant, on the sixth floor of Canada's most famous building.

In the Langevin Block, the mood was sombre.

In the boardroom, where he seldom went—he preferred his office in the Centre Block—Brian Mulroney was huddled with his top advisers, Finance Minister Wilson, Deputy Prime Minister Don Mazankowski and House Leader Doug Lewis.

The Boss listened to the gloom-and-doom scenario. Wilson had offered his resignation. Maybe they had no choice but to accept it. How big was the leak? Nobody knew.

Finally, exasperated and totally opposed to being forced into accepting the resignation of his minister, and the cancellation of his long-awaited budget, Mulroney put down his reading glasses and read them the riot act, "All right, Lewis, you're going to phone John Turner. And you are going to tell him we intend to bring back the Commons, because there has been a budget leak—and we intend to table it tonight."

Lewis apparently thought that his job was to persuade the Liberal leader to go along with the plan. But Mulroney had another idea, as he added, "If Turner is true to form, he'll say no. Let's hope he does."

Mulroney also told Lewis to write down what he intended to say to Turner, so as to avoid any mistakes. Interestingly enough, the next day, as the government was under attack, the Tory house leader would use those very same notes in the Commons, reading aloud exactly what he had told Turner on the phone that memorable night.

Mulroney then turned his guns on the second part of the strategy. "Wilson, you will call a press conference and release the budget, no lock-up, nothing, tonight."

That, of course, was depending on a refusal by the two opposition leaders to have a special House sitting, to let Wilson table the budget.

On that score, the plan worked. Turner and Broadbent did say no. The budget was given out prematurely at a press conference, as the media, without the benefit of a full day lock-up, stampeded through the National Press Building with all the purpose of a buffalo herd hit by mass hysteria.

Paradoxically, when it was all over the next day, and everybody had managed to get their stories filed on deadline, without having to sit in a locked room for several hours, most press gallery members agreed that this was the best budget they had ever had.

That attitude probably contributed to the fact that, although the media reported it, most were not too taken with the opposition's attack over the next few days, demanding Michael Wilson's resignation and holding up parliamentary debate.

Politics is very much a game of luck. Circumstances help you.

The media's relaxed attitude—including my own—had a lot to do with two things; first, as I mentioned earlier, the budget was out of the way more quickly than it had ever been. Second, this was the annual dinner week, and a lot of people's minds were more bent on social events than political fights. The media simply laid off, and didn't buy the indignation of the opposition.

It must be said that Turner and Broadbent had also blown it royally, though. First, they had let Michael Wilson hog most of prime time TV on April 26, when they should have taken over the airwaves by raising a stink in the Commons. Of course, their refusal to sit made that impossible.

When they finally got around to it, the next day, they forgot to tackle the very tough measures that were in the budget, and let the government get away with that, too.

Brian Mulroney got lucky.

When I met him on the following Saturday, at the press dinner, he was glowing. So much so, in fact, that we actually had a real conversation—but it must be said that, although he was evidently talking to me, he preferred to look at my guest. He obviously still wasn't ready to be perfectly normal with a "traitor."

He told me then how he had learned "crisis management," and how, five years before, "we wouldn't have known what to do."

Of course, he was referring to all the bungling of the three years I had worked with him, and how his handling of the budget leak affair had proven what he had learned.

He also told former adviser Bill Fox roughly the same

thing. Fox told me later, "The most amazing thing is not only that he talks about it, but he admits he didn't know crisis management himself."

He was right. Pride would have prevented Brian Mulroney from making such a frank assessment of himself in the early years.

However, for all his self-confidence, Mulroney had made a crucial mistake, which would return to haunt him in the weeks to come.

He had called the budget leak "a crime," and called in the RCMP to investigate. The Doug Small story was only beginning.

In the week that followed, I met with a governement friend. I shared with him my strong belief that they had no reason to worry about such an uncontrollable occurrence.

That person told me then, in a voice loaded with understatement, "You're right...if it's the only leak."

At the time, I took it as just another meaningless comment in a long conversation. But it came back to my memory when, in the following weeks, a "second" leak was discovered, thanks to the dogged persistence of an *Ottawa Sun* reporter by the name of Stuart McCarthy, who was determined to get to the truth before the politicians coloured it.

It's too bad we didn't find out about that leak before, because that one, had it been known on budget night, or in the days that followed, would have justified the resignation of Michael Wilson.

That one became known as the Mutual Life leak, as opposed to the Small leak. The government was told about it on April 27, when an official of Mutual Life phoned the finance minister's office, to say that an employee of theirs had had copies of the same budget-in-brief document, and that photocopies of the document had been made. The company made the call in order to act like a responsible corporate citizen.

This breach of secrecy was much more serious, though. A company of such magnitude can see advantages in a budget measure that are not evident to the naked eye. The RCMP investigators were more concerned about the possibility of Mutual Life profiting from the leak than they were about tracking down Doug Small's informer.

In fact, the RCMP believed that the Small leak, far from being profitable to the individuals involved—including the reporter—was actually instrumental in preventing other, less well-intentioned people from personally benefitting from advance knowledge of the budget.

I don't want to get into the details of the whole budget leak affair. To be done justice, it should be the subject of a whole book. Doug Small would be a perfect author.

The purpose of this chapter is, rather, to show how Brian Mulroney, when confronted with new evidence of a second budget leak—instead of coming right out with the truth—ordered his ministers to stonewall the opposition with a familiar line. "The whole thing is under police investigation."

Why? Because doing otherwise would have meant the end of Michael Wilson's career as finance minister.

Mulroney was then following a pattern that had gotten him into so much trouble in the past; burying the bodies, in the hope that they wouldn't be found. Fighting the truth with legal arguments. Admitting as little as possible until caught definitely.

Obviously, if he had learned crisis management, he still hadn't learned to cope with his greatest weakness. Politics is not a court of law. You don't win on a technicality. You win when people believe you are telling it like it is.

The worst was still to come.

After the revelation of the Mutual Life leak, came the greatest public relations blow of all. Doug Small was charged with possession of a stolen document.

It was laughable. The actual pamphlet Small had on the night of the budget fiasco was a discarded version, which had been sent to a paper recycling plant because the print wasn't right on it.

In fact, the police estimated that it was worth a fraction of one cent. But without charging Small, the Crown couldn't go after Appleby or the recycling plant worker who was alleged to have given him the budget-in-brief.

And the prime minister had said it was "a crime." If a crime had been committed, somebody was guilty and somebody had to pay. All this, of course, Mulroney had done simply to put the fear of God into anybody else who would dare leak budget information in the future. But did he intend to scare off a reporter who had simply done his job?

The prime minister learned of Small being charged in Brussels, where he was taking part in a NATO meeting after the Dakar Francophone Summit. His officials on the plane didn't know how to react, but felt they had a problem there.

In Ottawa, still a newsman in his heart, communications adviser Bruce Phillips said dejectedly, about the RCMP's decision to proceed against a reporter, "Well, thanks a lot..." He knew they had a problem.

With the summer of '89, it all sort of went away. Mulroney had put me in the deep freeze again, and avoided me like the plague after I wrote columns about his misguided use of our "Royal Canadian Mulroney Police." But it seemed that few people cared about it anymore.

As the fall came along, and the date of Small's trial grew nearer, the interest in it was still far from great. The media people, who would normally have been fascinated by it all, sort of shrugged at what was an "old story."

After all, that same week in October, Philippines President Corazon Aquino was coming to Ottawa. So were the first ministers, for a meeting aimed at settling problems about the Meech Lake Accord. In addition, the highly controversial abortion law was about to blow up again.

It was, indeed, a "Small" story.

I can't say that I was really any different from the rest. But I was still rather intrigued by it. And I became really fascinated after a lunch I had with somebody I can only call "a contact."

He told me, a few days before the beginning of the trial, that Small's defense counsel had information that was potentially very damaging for the government. I learned from another source that the leading RCMP investigator in the case was willing to testify that he didn't want to press charges against the Global reporter, but that his superiors had overruled him.

I really didn't believe something that dramatic would happen, as I walked to the Provincial Courtroom on Elgin street, that Monday morning. But I did share some of my information with colleague Tim Naumetz, who was covering the trial.

As it turned out, we didn't have to wait long for the dramatics.

Defense lawyer David Scott led off by asking Judge Jim Fontana to void the trial, because of "abuse of process." The defense motion maintained that charges had been laid in this case after undue political intervention and pressure. He called to the stand forty-one-year-old RCMP Staff Sergeant Richard Jordan, the chief investigator.

With the Crown prosecutor looking on in amazement at the police officer who was supposed to help him win his case, Jordan dropped the bomb: the case should never have come to trial.

Jordan revealed to a stunned courtroom that he had told RCMP Deputy Commissioner Henry Jensen that he did not think the evidence justified the laying of charges. He also quoted Jensen as saying that "journalists have to be taught a lesson." He thought that the whole case had been constructed "to please elected officials," and that the reasoning behind the charges, as expressed to him by a federal justice official was "bizarre."

From then on, the trial turned into a monumental farce, and Brian Mulroney had to defend himself against charges of political interference with the normal course of justice—a lot of the accusations coming from me.

In my columns, I reminded people of how the same prime minister had used the national police force to control the media, during the election campaign.

186

That earned me a heated discussion with Bruce Phillips, whom I consider to be an honourable man by any definition of the term. He said I was wrong, that neither the PM nor his office had ever interfered.

I told him that I had found out, when I was in the PMO, that sometimes even the prime minister's advisers were not being told the truth. He said, almost sadly, that that could very well be, but was highly improbable in this case.

I said that, even if he never gave the order directly, Mulroney had told the RCMP what to do the moment he declared a "crime" had been committed. Bruce could only nod at that. Not necessarily in agreement with my allegation, but because he knew the "crime" was now haunting the accuser, and not the perpetrator.

The prime minister's chief of staff, Stanley Hartt, was called to the stand, and so was his former executive assistant, Bill Pristanski, who had been the solicitor-general's chief of staff during the RCMP investigation. Their testimony didn't reveal much, other than that they were kept informed of the progress in the investigation on a regular basis, in case questions were asked in the Commons by the opposition.

Of course, when questions were asked, the government simply responded that an investigation was under way, and that it could not be jeopardized.

The Doug Small affair was a mess. Brian Mulroney had managed to turn what he thought was a strategic triumph into a disaster that further exposed his most flagrant flaw: lack of credibility.

Too cute by half, once again.

The Doug Small affair would not bring him or the government down, but it would enter the public subconscious as perhaps the greatest example of abuse of power and trust. When Brian Mulroney would need the people to believe him, perhaps they wouldn't be there.

**Chapter** 17

*Whooosh! Boiiing!*
*Whooosh! Boiiing!*

It was an incredibly sad and tragic sight. A telling symbol of man's self-destructive folly.

And Brian was stuck, looking at it before the cameras.

The magnificient bald eagle that should have been soaring two miles high was tied up by both legs, in a pound the size of a small city lot. A hunter's bullet in the left wing had condemned it to captivity, and made the proud bird totally dependent on man for its survival.

He could fly, but not very well, his handlers said. That assertion was a little hard to refute when you saw him tied to a six-foot rope, attached to a steel cable running the length of the lot about six inches off the ground. The apparatus was apparently designed to let the eagle fly "freely" from a roost at one end to his bird house—more like a dog house—about twenty metres away.

But the rope wouldn't often work as the designers planned it. As a result, whenever the bird would try to take off, it would get caught, and the eagle would be jolted back to the ground like a dog running full-speed to the end of its leash.

*Whoosh*, went the once-powerful wings. *Boiing*, went the cable. On and on as Yak—that was the eagle's name, as given by man—tried to fly away from his visitor, Mr. Yakety-Yak himself, Our Boy Brian.

This was all happening at the ecological centre of Port-au-Saumon, on the North Shore of the St. Lawrence in the prime minister's riding of Charlevoix, in July of '89.

This was photo-op time—something evidently chosen to illustrate the government's concern with the environment. Or was it their concern with pollsters? The environment was something Mulroney had discovered just prior to the 1988 election campaign. In 1984, with the theme of "jobs, jobs, jobs," we toured prosperous, government-funded, fish-packing plants. Five years later, we were visiting a centre that existed to save fish.

Whatever, Yak the Eagle, Miss Piggie the Falcon—in a neighbouring pound—and a horned owl two doors down were part of the Mulroney photo album that day.

Mulroney couldn't have been dumb enough to think that having him pose with a tied-up eagle, desperately looking for a place to hide from him and the throng of reporters and cameras, was actually a brilliant idea.

He had to wonder which one of his strategists had planned the outing this way.

With the eagle becoming an embarrassment for everyone watching, the prime minister was ushered next door to the falcon. One of the bird's handlers went inside the pound and prompted Miss Piggie to climb onto his extended arm. But when the falcon approached Brian, instead of standing upright, it was totally upside down and refusing to come up. It obviously didn't like what was going on.

We never saw the owl. He didn't come out of his house in the daytime.

But when it was all over, Yak got his reward. He was given his favourite dish—two dead partridges—which he tore to shreds for the gallery. Tasty.

Before meeting Yak, Mulroney had visited some dead birds in a nearby pavilion. They were part of a summer exhibit. Mulroney picked up one of the stuffed birds with a red crest, and joked that this was the only bird with a red head on the premises. Red, of course, means Liberal to Brian Mulroney, and he makes that kind of tiresome joke often.

This time he thought he would follow it up with an even worse groaner. Pointing to birds of a different colour, he said, "There are the bluebirds of happiness." All this while smiling widely at the camera.

One cameraman, who couldn't stand him any more, complained, "Who feeds him those lines?"

And that's precisely the point.

Mulroney, partly because his handlers sometimes put him in situations he can't handle properly, occasionally does and says strange things. He can't be loose because, for him, a perfect event is one that is totally controlled by his troops. Except that, when it goes off the rails—when a media scrum occurs, for instance—he doesn't know how to react.

All this contributes to the image of phoniness that he projects, as he seems to beg for the camera, instead of just letting things happen. I'm sure he didn't like to see the eagle tied up, any more than we in the media pack did. He should have said it, instead of joking about blue-birds of happiness.

He still doesn't understand that, following such events, the "boys" go out for dinner and make fun of him. Ridicule kills in politics. And his attempt at perfection in public outings also begs the media to find flaws in it, to try to break the cycle, to find a way to spoil the show. They simply won't let him get away with a photo op.

This kind of thing happened time and time again in the first mandate, when I was staging such events myself. We truly believed those who said the man had to have his "comfort zone." We didn't have a choice. If he didn't have it, he wouldn't blame himself, but us.

It didn't stop after his re-election. It seemed that every trip outside Ottawa—and outside the country—turned into a disaster or a joke, because of things largely out of his control. He has been incredibly unlucky that way.

Following are a few examples of unusual events that happened on such trips, in the short time I've been observing them from the other side, with some insights as to what was happening inside.

I've already told you about the Madame Tussaud Museum trip. Now, how about the one I call the Voyage of the Damned?

That was the trip Mulroney made, in the spring of '89, to Dakar, Senegal, for the third Francophone Summit, and then to Brussels, for a NATO meeting. I wasn't on the trip, but I got a full report from numerous people on both sides of the fence.

First, let's say the trip had an inherent problem. The first, and main, part of the outing meant very little to Canada's English media, who, of course, were the main components of the press pack travelling with the prime minister.

The Francophone Summit, by definition, does not generate much excitement for the editors back in Toronto or Vancouver, just as the Quebec media express very little interest in covering the Commonwealth Conference. It is perhaps one of the most blatant expressions of how truly divided our two solitudes are.

But the English contingent—although stripped to the bare essentials—still includes the representatives of the main media organizations. They are sent on a "death watch," in case something juicy or terrible happens, as often seems to be the case on Mulroney's trips.

This trip came right in the middle of the budget-leak crisis, as the RCMP investigation was about to be completed.

Adding to the low level of interest in the trip was the fact that Dakar is not the most enjoyable of cities. Except for the very rich, who shield themselves from the populace with elaborate security systems, it is a human sewer, where the starving Senegalese from the desert flock to escape famine and poverty, and end up in an overcrowded city where crime is often the only means of survival.

You see children without legs or with bandaged eyes begging on the streets, in scenes reminiscent of bible movies. You hear stories of parents deliberately maiming their children, to make effective beggars out of them. But even left uninjured, chances are that disease would get them anyway, in the infested universe of Dakar.

You do not walk the streets at night. People who are starving have little respect for human life, especially the white and rich, who represent their former colonial masters.

Now, the Mulroney people and travelling media were well shielded from those evils in their plush Meridien hotel, with the pool where the attractive Air France stewardesses would gather almost daily. The PMO's Jacques Labrie knew how to keep the boys happy.

But making them happy doesn't mean they don't get antsy. Sooner or later, they start feeling guilty. They begin to think of how much this trip costs, and how little they are doing to prove to their editors at the other end that it is worth sending them on another one.

So they were hungry for something to happen.

As often happens on international trips, the break came from Canada, not Senegal. That was when the second budget leak became known, and the desks back home wanted Mulroney's reaction to the renewed calls for Michael Wilson's resignation. Parliament was also ablaze with the scandal of Richard Grise, a Tory backbencher who had pleaded guilty to fraud charges earlier in the week, and who had the opposition screaming for his head.

The pack decided it was scrum time.

They had one chance to get to Mulroney early in the day, as he showed up with Quebec Premier Robert Bourassa to announce some joint book-funding project. At that point, though, they decided it would be impolite to intervene—believe it or not—and waited for another opportunity to strike later in the day.

Press Secretary Gilbert Lavoie told them it would

come later, as Mulroney visited a small fishing village where Canada's International Development Agency had made a substantial contribution. (Canadian politicians always tour these places when they go to Third World countries.)

But when Mulroney got to the village, his orders to his staff were quite different. Labrie and Gilbert Lavoie then got into a heated argument, as the Press Secretary tried to keep his promise of holding a scrum, but the more experienced press advance man (whom I had hired) told him The Boss would have nothing of it.

It was too late, though. The boys were already on the prowl, and would not be dissuaded.

As Mulroney walked through the village, trying to look casual and compassionate with his shades on, something else added a touch of weirdness and phoniness to the whole affair. With a phalanx of officials and media moving along with him, the prime minister was led through streets where fishing nets had been laid out to dry. When the crowd came through, the nets were torn to shreds, as screaming Senegalese fishermen jumped up and down to try and stop the carnage, all the time being pushed away by military police.

Through all this, one defiant Canadian reporter dared shout a question about Michael Wilson.

Mulroney had obviously rehearsed his response in his mind, as he had assuredly been told of the media ambush in advance. He said, indignantly, "Show a little class!"

That was when *The Toronto Star*'s Patrick Doyle shot back, "We wouldn't mind it if you would, sir!"

Mulroney could only stare back silently. He knew the reporter well. Like me, Doyle had worked for his government under minister Marcel Masse. He knew Mulroney, and he knew that "class" had nothing to do with his avoiding the media.

That night, on the national networks, that was all they would show of Mulroney's glorious trip to the Francophone Summit.

Quite an accomplishment. And it all came about because, on that given day, he thought he would use his planned photo op to avoid an already impatient media.

Dumb.

It didn't stop there. This whole merry bunch then flew off to Brussels for another showdown. Now, NATO is the Americans' show, and Canada is only a bit player there, looked down upon by other, more important members of the alliance, because of its small contribution to its defence forces.

That, coupled with the inexperience of Press Secretary Gilbert Lavoie, and the Dakar encounter, created much bitterness within the Canadian press corps. They were being scooped left and right by the Americans, the French and the British, as Canadian officials refused to give briefings.

It was veteran Presse Canadienne reporter Pierre April, otherwise known lovingly as the Hill's Tasmanian Devil, who finally blew up at the Mulroney staff. He was fed up with being told by his Montreal desk that the French service had filed the same story he was trying to sell, several hours earlier. Poor Gilbert Lavoie was on the receiving end of the verbal attack—something quite memorable, I'm told.

Things improved after that. But there was still the long flight home.

That was when the Voyage of the Damned earned its name.

Pat Doyle, for one, now says in retrospect that "it probably wasn't as bad as it seemed at the time." But when they got off that airplane, the stories about the trip back were some of the wildest to be spread through this incestuous town in years.

First there was the physical altercation between April and Lavoie, as the reporter grabbed the press secretary by the scruff of the neck and told him exactly what was on his mind. What provoked the incident is quite irrelevant. The fact that it even happened is a clear sign that the pressure on that trip had reached unbearable proportions.

*Sun* reporter Tim Naumetz was then caught smoking in the washrooms; a no-no on any flight.

The same man also got into an argument with *La Presse*'s star columnist, Lysianne Gagnon. Whatever it was he said, she burst out in tears on the prime minister's airplane, and had to be comforted by Telemedia reporter Yves Bellavance.

In was a raucous, angry trip home, with lots of drinking involved.

Pierre April almost lost his job over it, as the Toronto bosses descended on him. The PMO intervened, to say it hadn't been all that bad, but only served to confirm the incident.

All in all, it was ugly. And I personally believe that a lot of it was prompted by the confrontational and secretive attitude Mulroney himself displayed with a press that was just trying to do its job.

I know, because I saw it happen more than once, while I was working for him. We were always torn between our loyalty to him, our desire to please, and the media's needs. We never reached a good balance while I was there, and often paid a heavy price.

Now, to another one of the Great Leader's daring international ventures, the Paris Economic Summit that coincided with the grandiose celebrations of the French Revolution's bicentennial.

It wasn't so much the trip itself that caused the prime minister aggravation this time. It was what took place before, when Canada scrambled to find a suitable gift to offer to France on this memorable occasion.

In this case, it was a painting. A $1.5 million Jean-Paul Riopelle mural.

On this occasion, Mulroney had little to do with the embarrassment other people caused for him. But that, again, seemed to follow a disturbing pattern.

The problem was that the Riopelle in question was already hanging in a Canadian building, at Toronto's Pearson Airport, when the government decided to take it off the wall and give it to the French.

Since Canada had only paid $20,000 in 1963, when it commissioned the world-renowned Canadian artist to do it, nobody bothered assessing the work at its present market value. Had they done so, chances are the decision to rip it from the wall of the airport and give it to the Paris Bastille Opera House would not have been made.

There are some within the Mulroney entourage who contest the $1.5 million evaluation. Well, if it wasn't worth that before Canada gave it away, it's assuredly worth a hell of a lot more now, after all the trouble it caused and the publicity it got.

The funniest part of this story is the reason why the painting was chosen. It was not the result of some careful planning and screening from our Canadian officials at External Affairs or the PMO. It was a last-minute affair.

We did to France what a forgetful husband does to his wife at 5:00 p.m. when, coming home from work, he suddenly remembers it's their wedding anniversary.

In fact, the PMO people were shocked, when they did the advance work for the trip, to find out so little had been done by the diplomats, who still hadn't come up with a proper gift in April, less than three months before the event.

Since the gift was intended to be a fitting art product, it had to be commissioned—and it simply had to be created!

The diplomats' brainstorm was to give bronze doors for the Opera House. But the doors couldn't be completed before the opening. Somebody suggested that Mulroney could "promise" the doors. Brilliant. The prime minister would have ended up going to the official opening of a building left unfinished, thanks to Canada's tardiness.

Somebody suggested a statue. Again, no time.

Finally, some "expert" thought of the "useless" Riopelle at the Pearson terminal. What a bargain that was. Already done and all.

Of course, on top of ignoring the price of the painting, they never imagined that the artist would express some concern over the way his work was being treated.

Riopelle, living in France and described as "a recluse," commented on the Canadian government's actions through his daughter Yseult, saying that a painting should remain in the place it was originally created for.

When I raised a stink about the whole affair, the PMO told me they had a letter on file from Riopelle saying he was very happy with the fact that his painting would be exposed in France.

Fine. But I know of such letters. Very often, they are requested by the government to cover its ass. I suspect, given the reaction of the artist's daughter, that this one was one of those.

To add to the embarrassment, the government actually contravened at least the spirit of one of its own laws, intended to protect national art treasures. It was passed in 1977, and makes it very difficult for any private entrepreneur to bleed Canada of its cultural heritage.

Although the painting does not officially fall under the law, because the artist is still living, that's getting away on a mere technicality. Mulroney didn't even know such a law existed, when he was told what gift he was handing to France.

The ultimate argument for Mulroney's apologists in this matter was to say that, had it been a gift to the U.S. or to the British monarch, such a fuss would not have been raised. They certainly have a point. There are people in this country who go crazy when we give Chuck and Di a jade horse or Ronald Reagan a swayback. It's a desperate argument to explain a total screw-up.

That's to be expected when Mulroney goes overseas. Ask Madame Tussaud.

And it's not going to stop Brian from trying. A few months later, he was back on the Boeing 707, on his way to the Commonwealth Conference in Malaysia—with a stop-over in Singapore—and a concluding trip to Costa Rica, where he would rub elbows with George Bush and the leaders of Latin American countries.

Trouble came unexpectedly in Kuala Lumpur, Malaysia.

The leaders of the Commonwealth had apparently agreed on a declaration, whereby sanctions against South

Africa should be maintained, despite President de Klerk's reforms, until apartheid was forever abolished. The matter of sanctions against that country have been the main topic of discussion at the Commonwealth Conferences ever since Mulroney came to power, in 1984. He has been a strong supporter of them, and was instrumental in bridging the gap between Great Britain's Margaret Thatcher—staunchly opposed to sanctions—and the smaller countries of the old British Empire.

He believed the same thing had been accomplished in Malaysia, after he agreed to sign the declaration. He thought Margaret was on side.

Nevertheless, he sent some of his officials to check on the British briefing of what had transpired. He was relieved when they came back saying there was "nothing to it."

He was consequently stunned, when confronted later with the fact that Maggie had basically broken with the Commonwealth and said she didn't approve of the joint communique.

Mulroney, for the first time since his election, then tried to get into a shouting match, through the press, with the leader of an allied country. But he was ill-prepared, because he had been misinformed on what the British had told their press corps.

Margaret Thatcher laughed him off, and appeared defiant as she claimed that if it was one against the rest that was fine with her.

The Canadian media were sympathetic to Mulroney's cause, but it was evident that the strong-willed Maggie had won the day.

Still, the prime minister was in a jovial mood as he headed back across the Pacific to Costa Rica. He came to the back of the plane to chat with "the boys." So often, in fact, that they started saying, "Oh no, not him again..."

Of course, it was a form of group bravado for the media to react in such a way. They are as ambivalent toward Mulroney as he is toward them. Most of them still can't force themselves to truly hate the man, and they are all curious about seeing him up close. It's too bad, though, that even in relaxed circumstances, the relations between Mulroney and the "other side" are so tense.

The prime minister flew into the capital, San Jose, confident that the most difficult part of his trip was behind him. The upcoming meeting was the one where Nicaraguan President Daniel Ortega would provoke the wrath of President George Bush, by announcing an end to the ceasefire with the Contras, while in Costa Rica to discuss peace in the region.

That, of course, would overshadow Canada's big planned announcement that it was joining the U.S.-controlled Organization of American States—something the Department of External Affairs had been advising the government against for years.

But that wasn't Brian's main problem. His tuxedo was.

He was to attend a major reception given by his Costa Rican host, along with other participants in the meeting. His staff told him it was a black-tie event. He didn't think twice, as he donned his silk shirt, cummerbund and bow tie and headed for the ball at the palace, better dressed than Cinderella. He might as well have been a pumpkin.

In fact, he was better suited than anybody else, except the waiters. It was not a black-tie event and it was too late to turn back.

Needless to say, the man, who is fussy about the dress code when he goes to a baseball game, was not amused as he looked around to see, for instance, Daniel Ortega in his battle fatigues—which he called a "boy scout outfit."

But the most hurtful part of it all came when George Bush's chief of staff walked by, and said with a smirk, "Hi, Brian! Did you bring your orchestra?"

It couldn't happen to a better guy.

On a more serious note, Mulroney was also ridiculed because our RCMP security forces decided to fly down his armoured limousine to Costa Rica. The matter was raised in the Commons after his trip, by Liberal MP Len Hopkins. The Neanderthal MP was trying to make fun of Mulroney's presidential style in flying down a limo that couldn't even be used.

It all started in a very innocuous way, as a story appeared on the Southam News Service about the use of the limo. It made fun of the fact that it couldn't run down there, because they had no unleaded gasoline.

The facts were quite different. First of all, the limousine could have run on leaded gas, as most cars can, if need be. Secondly, the RCMP security forces, who had scouted the area first, knew no unleaded gas was available, and had a half-tank of Canadian gas, which was much more than they could possibly need for the short rides and the short stay.

More importantly, though, Mulroney's life had been threatened by the Columbian drug lords.

A letter had been sent to the PMO and the CBC news service in Toronto, a few weeks before the PM's visit to Central America. This was never made known to the public. It was not one of those "wacko" letters. It actually outlined how Brian Mulroney had been picked as a target by the drug lords. It seemed authentic. The author of the letter explained that the would-be assassins thought Bush would be too hard a prey to get at. They were ready to settle for Mulroney.

The Mounties, accustomed to this sort of nonsense, took it seriously. The fact that other letters backed up the first one reinforced their belief that, perhaps, this was for real.

They put it to the PMO people. Do we fly down the limousine?

The Mounties asked them because they knew of the negative political implications for a prime minister who had been highly criticized for his royal travelling style.

But there was even more than that. The RCMP was so concerned about the threat that, for the first time ever, they wanted to take arms into a foreign country. Remember, this is something they do not officially let other security forces do—not even the American Secret Service—when their leaders travel to Canada. (Although everybody in the VIP force knows that most foeign security agents, using diplomatic passports, manage to get their weapons into the country and carry them on their bodies when the time comes to protect the leader.)

The deployment of RCMP forces in Costa Rica, however, was phenomenal, compared to everything else we have known before in a foreign country, where their numbers rarely exceed six. They had as many as forty officers—some say seventy—in a city that was already swarming with American Secret Service people. In fact, as the story goes, Bush's bodyguards had even taken over the air traffic control at the city's airport.

Officially, our police kept their arms within the Canadian embassy compound, where the prime minister resided. But they actually had them everywhere they went with the prime minister and his staff.

Mulroney of course, could have decided to do without the protection. But the adviser who was given the RCMP recommendation for decisive action had to make a decision between protecting a public relations image or protecting a man's life.

"What would you have done?" he asked me.

I would have done exactly what they did, and taken the heat for it.

But, once again, it was too late to repair the damage. I knew the feeling well. Once the story was finished, who cared about catch-up explanations? And besides, Mulroney, in his stubborn pride, didn't want to be seen as the prime minister who needed protection from the big bad guys. In the end, he ended up unfairly looking worse.

But that didn't stop Our Boy Brian's globe-trotting habits. He had a date in the USSR a few weeks later, and he intended to keep it.

It was possibly the most impressive international outing he had made since his 1984 election, and it happened at a time when the whole Eastern Bloc was undergoing a democratic revolution that went beyond anybody's imagination or predictions.

Although there were some who said he was meeting

with Mikhail Gorbachev at least two years too late, when the Soviet leader least needed him, Mulroney claimed that he "couldn't think of a more interesting place to be in than Moscow tomorrow."

As confident as he may have seemed then, he was really doing a good job of hiding his anxieties about the trip and other things.

Let's talk about the "other things" first.

As he hit the trail for the USSR, Brian Mulroney was a very lonely man. After the three-week trip to Asia and Costa Rica, he had come back to Canada to a difficult and controversial first ministers' conference on the Meech Lake Accord, which forewarned of the national break-up lurking seven months down the road. The GST communications strategy was a mess, his friend, Senator Michel Cogger, was in hot water with the law, and the Doug Small trial was a disaster.

Through it all, Brian Mulroney felt he had no support from his cabinet ministers.

"He has to do everything himself," one of his confidants told me. "He gets no help from his ministers on anything. Not Meech Lake, not the GST, nothing!"

But there was more. Mulroney felt let down by his own office. Chief of Staff Stanley Hartt didn't have control of the operations and, as my informant told me, was "more preoccupied with babying Michael Wilson on the GST" than with doing his job and getting the PMO to work. The Press Office was there only in name, as Press Secretary Gilbert Lavoie appeared unable to cope with the hard realities of a sudden change of life from journalism to politics.

The problem was so real that, at the end of the first ministers' conference that week, Mulroney instinctively asked a man named Ronald Poupart if he would please go and see "what the boys are saying."

Poupart was one of Quebec Premier Robert Bourassa's main advisers. Being naturally affable, he obliged. But the absurdity of the situation wasn't lost on him. When a prime minister has to ask a premier's aide to do something as routine as finding out what the press is up to, it is a disturbing sign of a much more profound malaise.

Mulroney had reason to be worried. Two months before his trip to the USSR—possibly the most crucial international visit of his mandate—he couldn't get straight answers from his top aides on what was going on out there.

Fed up, he called on his number-one trouble-shooter, Luc Lavoie, to do the job. With very little time left before the visit, Mulroney sent him to the Soviet Union, to make it happen.

Lavoie got carte blanche, and took it from there.

He brought with him his right-hand man, Jacques Labrie, and they set out on an advance trip. The two PMO staffers, exceptionally, took along a CBC producer, Halina St. James, for the trip, since they knew television connections would be difficult. Of course, she wasn't expected to use anything she learned on the trip, on the news. She was there strictly "for planning purposes."

This cooperation with news operations on advance trips was something Bill Fox and I had experimented with in the PMO, but this was the first time somebody from the Mother Corp. had gone along on an advance trip, as part of a PMO delegation.

I learned about her going as we were going up the elevator of the National Press Building at 150 Wellington. It happened to be the day I was filing my Friday "gossip" column—a collection of tidbits you can't turn into a full-fledged rant—and I thought it was a good item.

So did the Russians.

The Lavoie-Labrie duo never expected what the Soviets dropped on them next.

As they sat down with officials in Moscow to organize their advance trip, one pointed out that Halina St. James could not go along, because she was a journalist.

When the PMO boys protested, the Russians produced a briefing book.

Labrie, who could see what they had from across the table, asked Lavoie, "Do you see what I see?"

"Yeah..."

"Do you believe it?"

"No."

For those two, seeing a copy of my column in a Soviet briefing book was like seeing a copy of *Mad* magazine used as evidence against their case because, for years, Lavoie, Labrie and I had been drinking buddies—most of those occasions, of course, had come before their PMO days.

Trying not to burst out laughing, they skated around the issue, like Alexander Yakushev around Serge Savard, and managed to get their producer on the plane.

They also managed to get Mulroney's show on the road.

In the end, it was a good trip. Certainly the most fascinating I took with the prime minister, on either side of the political fence.

Mulroney did well, I suppose.

I frankly did not pay much attention to what he was doing. I was too busy finding out about the society around me in Moscow, Kiev and Leningrad. I came away with the belief that the challenge facing Mikhail Gorbachev was beyond human abilities.

I shared that with the prime minister on the way back, as he strolled down the aisle of the airplane and chatted with us.

He agreed with me totally, and I could sense the admiration he felt for the Soviet leader.

It was a nice conversation, as short as it was. It reminded me of the last trip I took with him to Africa. Another fascinating venture, where I had finally decided my PMO days were over, without sharing it with the prime minister.

His government was in deep trouble then, hovering around twenty-two percent in the polls after the latest scandal—the Oerlikon affair. But we had the mellowest exhange we'd ever had, as if nothing really mattered all that much anymore.

For some reason, I had that feeling on the way back from the Soviet Union.

So much for sentiment. We had to keep on trekking.

So, once we got over the Christmas holidays, Brian, a few of the boys and girls and I took the government jet down to a warmer climate than the Canadian February Blues were providing. We spent an extended long week-end in Mexico and Barbados.

What crazy thing happened down there?

Well, apart from the fact that the prime minister was preoccupied with trying to solve the Meech Lake Accord deadlock, not much, in the political sense.

They wouldn't even tell us that the whole visit to Mexico was aimed at gaining our support for a free-trade deal between that country and the U.S.—although everybody else was telling us that was what it was all about.

Frankly, my dear, we didn't give a damn. This was truly a death watch. And the PMO had done everything to downplay the visit—including cutting our leisure time down there, so we couldn't write stories about how Mulroney was taking it easy on taxpayers money.

Oh, there was this story about how Mulroney had forgiven a $182-million debt to the Commonwealth countries of the Caribbean, which apparently caused quite a stir back home with the red-neck crowd.

It didn't matter that the debt probably would never have been recovered anyway. This was just another chance to kick Mulroney: he was giving away our money to Third World countries, while we needed it at home.

It made good headlines, I suppose.

But all in all, the trip was rather uneventful. Even the flight back from Barbados was unusually calm. For once, I thought, Mulroney had gotten away with an international outing without falling on his own sword.

But we weren't home yet...

What happened when we landed at Ottawa's military airport that night was something every Canadian citizen should have witnessed. Because it was pretty scary, and it gave us a good idea of how fragile freedom can be, even in our land, if we leave too much power to the military or the police.

It is hard to know exactly what happened at the

arrival—which should have been just another routine operation—to provoke the ugly scene that took place.

This is the view from my vantage point.

First of all, it had been a very quiet flight home. Nothing like the Voyage of the Damned. No heavy drinking, no partying, no fighting. It was also a relatively small press contingent, since several members of the travelling media had stayed back to enjoy a holiday in Barbados.

All in all, a very easy group to handle under any circumstances.

When we landed, we followed normal procedure, exiting through the rear door of the Boeing 707, along with most of the PMO and External Affairs staffers.

As I stepped out the back door, after about twenty other passengers, things came to a sudden stop. Somebody in a military uniform was blocking our passage at the bottom of the ramp.

The PMO's Jacques Labrie was there, screaming and flailing his arms, trying to get the military police to let us through. They, in turn, kept saying that we had to go through customs.

Nobody argued that. But, according to normal procedure, the travelling press should have been allowed to go to the front ramp of the airplane, to make sure the prime minister didn't say or do anything before getting into his limousine.

I had done enough of these arrivals, on both sides of the fence, to know.

Now the craziest fact in all this is that very few of us actually wanted to go to the front of the aircraft. We just wanted to go through customs and go home.

But the military were blocking the bottom of the ramp.

I pushed my way to the bottom, to try and help out Labrie, hoping my experience in these matters would be useful. As it turned out, my arrival probably contributed to the panic that ensued, as the military police called for reinforcements.

Now everybody was screaming on the ground, as the

soldiers—kids mostly—looked on in total amazement, eyes glazed and mouths opened. They obviously had no idea who they were dealing with, and were treating us like just so many drunken sailors in a Halifax bar.

Labrie did something he then lived to regret. He called on another one of the PM's aides, Jean-Maurice Duplessis, to come over and help him put some sense into the military. The problem was, Duplessis was at the front ramp, since he was helping the prime minister deplane.

When he walked over, the soldiers didn't know where he had come from. When he tried to go back to the front ramp, which the military had made off-limits, they stopped him.

He then started to scream himself, trying to push his way through.

Then a soldier yelled an order. "Take him away!"

What followed was something I never thought—or hoped—I would live to see in my country.

The military police literally jumped Duplessis and wrestled him to the ground.

While the PMO staffer screamed "Somebody do something!" one police officer kicked his head into the ground, while another handcuffed him behind his back. The commander of the aircraft came running over and bent down to try and help Duplessis—knowing who he was—but the police, ignoring his uniform, threatened him too.

At that point, I walked over to the man and told him, "It's too late. He's got the cuffs on. We'll settle it inside."

The incident did nothing to calm things down, as insults flew furiously, with a normally mild-mannered person like *The Toronto Star*'s David Vienneau screaming at the top of his lungs that this was worse than Romania.

The military then threatened to take PMO staffer Jacques Labrie away too, if he didn't shut up. At that point, it came very close to an all-out brawl. I still don't know why it didn't happen. And in my heart, I still feel guilty about not having done anything more drastic than talk.

After they dragged Duplessis away, the screaming

crowd of reporters followed in pursuit, inside the airport terminal.

We weren't happy, but the man in the handcuffs was in even sadder shape. The soldiers shoved him heavily into the base commander's office. To make sure it hurt, one of them grabbed the chain of the handcuffs as they pushed him. That's the sort of thing they do to rowdy soldiers.

An RCMP bodyguard, who had just walked in, shouted "Whoooah!" to the military police. He knew what they were up to. Feisty PMO senior adviser Luc Lavoie then got into the act, and put one of the soldiers up against the wall in the commanding officer's office. The soldier went for his gun. The RCMP stared him down. The soldier left his weapon in the holster.

Another RCMP bodyguard stormed into the office. He was a big one, a natural figure of authority. "What's going on here?" he shouted.

That sort of calmed things down.

Duplessis was asked to give his version of the story.

He started to relate it in French, the language he is most comfortable in—the one you use when your freedom is on the line.

But one of the arresting officers, with a very heavy French accent, said to him, "Speak English please. This is a bilingual country and in a bilingual country, when somebody does not understand French, you speak English."

Only one officer in the place didn't speak French and, in a twist of irony that could only happen in Canada, it was he who said, "Parlez francais s'il-vous-plait."

Thanks mostly to the RCMP intervention, Duplessis was sprung quickly. But not before being uselessly humiliated, having his watch broken and his forehead cut.

All this of course, was totally unwarranted—except perhaps, as Vienneau said, in countries like Romania.

After all, this was a Mulroney trip. Something bad had to happen somewhere.

But, for Brian, the most painful ride was still to come.

**Chapter 18**

He heard about the telegram on the radio. It was about 1:00 a.m. on Saturday, May 19, 1990.

Brian Mulroney's greatest dream had just died. And he was going to lose a friend in the process.

*No, not him,* he thought.

Life had not been easy nor peaceful these last few weeks for the battered prime minister. In an ugly twist of fate that comes only in Canadian politics, the "national reconciliation" he had talked about with so much fervour and pride, just six years before, had become a symbol of division in the land he was elected to unite.

The Meech Lake Accord. Even he had come to hate the name. He wished he could have changed it, he wished he could have explained it, he wished he didn't have to be second-guessing himself.

There was no more "honour and enthusiasm" left for Quebec's re-entry into Canada's constitutional fold. The words he had spoken now sounded so hollow, almost ridiculous. The country was breaking up, and he knew he would be blamed for it. He had only one solution left, and he didn't like it. He had to ram it through, damn the torpedoes. There was no more glory left in this. It just had to be done. The Meech Lake Accord! God, he wished he'd never touched it.

Just two months earlier, he had jumped through what he thought was his "window of opportunity."

He was in Mexico City at the time. The phone call came from Frank McKenna, the premier of New Brunswick.

The man who had started the whole Meech Lake opposition had a plan to get the country out of the mess. He called it a "companion accord."

Mulroney was troubled. Here he was, meeting with President Salinas, when he should have been back home saving the country. He was here talking about some remote free-trade deal between the U.S. and Mexico, when he wanted to be in Ottawa salvaging whatever was left of the accord.

Brian Mulroney was playing high stakes, but he was at the wrong card game.

The McKenna proposal really got him going. He scanned through his Mexico briefing books but, when he called on his advisers, it was to talk about Meech Lake. What should he do?

All along, he had sided with Quebec's contention that Meech Lake, as it was, could not be changed, that it was the bottom line.

Political reality had intervened in the meantime, however, and he knew that somebody—everybody—had to move a little, or else...

McKenna's proposal did not look like a retreat or defeat to him. It looked, rather, like an apology from a premier who was trying desperately to save face, after finally understanding that Quebec was serious in its intention to go it alone, should Meech fail.

Maybe he finally had the opening he had been looking for.

He got on the phone to Ottawa. When he came back from Mexico, he wanted to talk Meech Lake. He thought of creating a parliamentary committee, but he knew where the problem lay: Quebec. How would his Quebec ministers and MPs take it? How would Bourassa take it?

He thought he could deal with Bourassa because, like him, the Quebec premier was, above all, a pragmatic politician. But how would Lucien Bouchard take it? He had that romantic streak. He didn't understand politics too well. Bah! Lucien would understand, once Meech Lake passed anyway. A calculated risk.

In a daze, he travelled to Barbados where, for the first time, he indicated to the stunned media, travelling along more for a winter holiday than for great news interest, that there might be a breathrough in the Meech Lake impasse.

Nobody in the suntanned press pack suspected what the prime minister had up his sleeve.

He went back to his hotel suite and asked his aides what they thought of him going on TV to make a national address on the Meech Lake Accord, after McKenna had made his own announcement.

At this point in the game, everybody thought action was better than nothing.

The ball had started to roll. But where was it going?

Mulroney returned to Canada—and to the military police reception I referred to earlier. He faced strong reservations about setting up a parliamentary committee to salvage Meech, from the predictable sources—his Quebec ministers. His personal friend Lucien was, of course, the most adamant. Any dilution of the accord was unacceptable to Quebec.

Mulroney knew that. But he also thought that there was a way to get Meech through, along with what McKenna called a companion accord, without selling out, or appearing to sell out, Quebec. He asked Lucien to give him a chance. In the end, it was better than nothing.

It almost worked.

Mulroney arrived in Ottawa on March 20. The next day, Frank McKenna publicly announced his intention to compromise, as he had put it to the prime minister several days before.

A couple of days later, Mulroney started working on his speech to the nation.

It wasn't easy. He got several drafts, but wasn't happy with any one of them.

Sitting in his den at 24 Sussex, he despaired of finding the words he needed to speak to Canadians. He wanted to touch their hearts. He struggled. He went to bed on the night of March 25, with a still-unfinished script. The taping of the speech was set for the next day.

When he finally did it, it was not as inspiring as he would have wished it. Rather, it was loaded with the uncertainty that was starting to grip both him and the country.

He appointed Tory MP Jean Charest as chairman of the special committee. It was his way of "rehabilitating" the young and flashy Charest, who had been forced to resign from his sports minister portfolio a few months earlier, because he had phoned a judge.

Officially, he couldn't give any direction to the committee. But, in fact, Mulroney—through his aides—was part of the strategy all along.

The first part of that strategy was relatively easy. The committee had to submit its report in a hurry.

The second part was a little trickier: somehow, they had to get Jean Chretien—whom everybody knew was about to become Liberal leader—on side.

Why? Because Chretien was their only hope of ever getting both Newfoundland Premier Clyde Wells and Manitoba's Liberal Opposition Leader Sharon Carstairs to agree to the Meech accord.

In Mulroney's machiavellian mind, this all made terrific sense.

However, his Quebec lieutenant, Lucien Bouchard, didn't think so.

For two months the pot kept boiling, as the whole country raced to the edge of the Meech Lake precipice.

One week before the committee was to submit its report, Mulroney had a crucial meeting with his key constitutional players.

On May 11, he called to 24 Sussex Senator Lowell

Murray, his federal-provincial minister, Stanley Hartt, his chief of staff, Paul Tellier, the Clerk of the Privy Council and Norman Spector, secretary to the cabinet for federal-provincial affairs.

As important as the meeting was, it was what Brian Mulroney was to say about it, a little more than one month down the road, that would immortalize it in Canadian history.

The main reason for the gathering was to set the strategy for possibly calling a full-fledged first ministers' conference, to solve the Meech Lake impasse. They had very little time left, before the June 23 constitutional deadline.

The first thing Mulroney asked for was a legal opinion on how solid that deadline was. So far, he had accepted it mainly as a "political" deadline. Now he wanted to know for sure if, somehow, the constitutional requirement could be bent.

The legal advice was firm. The deadline was exactly that.

Once he knew that, Mulroney looked at the calendar.

His aides suggested holding the conference on Friday, May 25. Mulroney didn't like it. He had telexes from his ambassador in Moscow, telling him that Mikhail Gorbachev might make an official visit to Canada during the week of the 27th, before his meeting with George Bush.

There was no big deal to the visit, as such. Gorbachev merely wanted some "down-time" to recover from jetlag, before going on to the serious part of his trip in Washington. But you do not pass up an opportunity to meet with the man who could be the most important political figure of the last fifty years. And you don't pass up a photo opportunity with Gorby. That's like turning down Brooke Shields for a date.

So, the prime minister didn't like the date of May 25.

His aides argued that it still gave him a full weekend to hold the first ministers' meeting. Mulroney scoffed at the suggestion.

"It took Trudeau a full week, in '81," he pointed out,

referring to the constitutional conference that had culminated in the patriation of the constitution, and the exclusion of Quebec.

His chief of staff, Stanley Hartt, suggested that perhaps the conference could go on during Gorbachev's visit, if need be.

Mulroney thought it was lunacy.

The most important part of the equation, to him, was Manitoba. Tory Premier Gary Filmon, being in a minority government situation, had less manoeuvring room than anybody else at the bargaining table. Even if they should strike a deal in Ottawa, he still had to get it through a legislature that wouldn't necessarily cooperate.

Mulroney called him and asked him exactly how many days he needed, "if we get a deal."

The prime minister swears Filmon told him thirteen days. The Manitoba premier denied later that he had ever made such a statement. Since there are no known tape recordings of the conversation, I suppose we will never know what was said.

After having established that, Mulroney then looked at the calendar, and "counted backwards." Remember those two words, because they came back to haunt the prime minister. He counted backwards thirteen days from June 23. That brought him to June 9. He pointed at a date on the calendar, where he said he was going to "roll all the dice."

That was Sunday, June 3.

The prime minister's advisers packed up their briefcases.

A week later, on May 17, the Charest committee submitted its report. It had, as Lucien Bouchard would comment later, Jean Chretien's fingerprints all over it.

Mulroney did not repudiate it.

Now on that Saturday morning of May 19, listening to the news on the radio about the Parti Quebecois meeting in Alma, Quebec, he heard about "the telegram."

Jacques Parizeau, the leader of Quebec's separatist party, was reading a telegram he had just received from Paris, France. It had been sent by the MP for Alma,

Lucien Bouchard, to commemorate—like the PQ gathering—the tenth anniversary of Quebec's referendum on separation, which had ended up in a victory for the *No* side.

The telegram was a vibrant endorsement of Quebec's right to self-determination. Bouchard reminded everyone of how he had worked for the *Yes* side during the referendum campaign, and those who did had to be proud of it. It didn't sound at all like a letter coming from a federal minister. Not the type we were used to, anyway.

So much so, in fact, that Parizeau had decided to read it out loud to his crowd of supporters, who broke out into wild applause, taking Bouchard's telegram as a vote of approval for the separatist cause.

Mulroney was beside himself.

How could Lucien be that stupid?

He got on the phone to his advisers, and told them to track down the minister, in Paris.

Luc Lavoie, Mulroney's TV guru, who had struck up a personal friendship with Bouchard since the by-election in Lac St-Jean two years earlier, was picked to do the dirty job of intermediary.

The suspense lasted all weekend, as the national press jumped on the story of Bouchard—highlighting, of course, his well-known separatist tendencies.

Lavoie was going through hell, trying to get Bouchard to backtrack. Lucien didn't want to. He'd had it with Ottawa and English Canada. He was walking.

Mulroney was like a caged lion at 24 Sussex. First there was the rage, a rage only he is capable of. When he gets like that, even his closest long-time friends become scumbags. And that's exactly what he thought of Lucien at that time.

He then went through a period when he almost laughed about it all. How naive Lucien was! He always had been.

But through the whole thing, the strongest feeling was one of immense sadness. Because Brian Mulroney knew what had to be done. Yes, he would give Lucien one more chance to take back what he said, but he knew the answer to that. And the next move was plain and simple: his friend had to go.

Bouchard landed at Mirabel airport the next Sunday night. He didn't retract any of his statements when confronted by the press.

That same night, I called someone I thought would know what on earth was going on because, like everybody else with half a brain, I realized something big was in the making. I must admit, however, that I thought Mulroney would do everything in his power not to drop Lucien.

I asked my informant what was going on. He was unusually discreet about it, saying only, "I know what's happening, but I can't tell you."

When I asked him if Lucien Bouchard was going to resign, he didn't answer. "Silence," was all he said.

When I asked him if something would happen publicly the next day, I got the same response.

It was around midnight on Sunday. I hung up the phone and told my wife, Christine, "Something big is happening on this Bouchard thing..."

The next day, the prime minister asked to see his rebellious minister. He didn't want to request his resignation by proxy. That was not the way Brian Mulroney did business. Again, it was Lavoie's job to arrange that, although he disapproved of the meeting, thinking it would produce an unnecessary blow-up between the two long-time friends.

Lucien told Lavoie he didn't think a meeting was a good idea. Luc agreed and relayed the message back to Mulroney, along with his own recommendation that he thought Bouchard was right.

The prime minister would have none of it.

Lavoie sighed, and got on the phone to Bouchard again. "Look, Lucien, he won't change his mind. He wants to see you."

Bouchard took a deep breath too, but thought he owed it to Brian. He would go to 24 Sussex, where his other old friend, Bernard Roy, was also present—Mulroney had him come down from Montreal.

Bouchard went into a closed-door meeting with Mulroney, expecting the worst. He knew Brian's temper.

To his great surprise, the prime minister was extremely calm.

They discussed briefly the possibility of his taking back some of the things he had said in the telegram. Lucien said he couldn't and that, in any case, he couldn't agree with the concessions offered in the Charest committee report.

Mulroney nodded, and said simply, "In that case, I will have to ask for your resignation."

"I was about to offer it," replied Lucien.

The prime minister then looked at him, and added, "Lucien, you may just have killed Meech Lake. But you are my friend. We have been friends for thirty years. You are still and will always be my friend."

To Bouchard's great surprise, Mulroney then provided him with advice. He didn't want him to "look like a fool" in the course of his resignation. "If you're going to resign, do it right," he said.

Bouchard left 24 Sussex at about 9:00 p.m., more impressed with Brian Mulroney than he had ever been.

The prime minister shut the door and got on the phone to Luc Lavoie to discuss matters of state.

A distraught Lavoie told him, "You know, sir, over the last two days, I have been in a very difficult situation. I feel like shit. Lucien is my friend—my true friend. You're my boss, because I chose to work for you, and I have never regretted it. But it's been hard."

"Don't worry, mon Luc. I know it's hard for all of us," said Mulroney. "Your boss is looking ahead...and Canada's not dead yet."

Ominous words.

Mulroney had already figured out that, as much as Bouchard's departure could kill Meech Lake, it could possibly shake English Canada's torpor, and make the dissident premiers understand that Quebec, indeed, meant business.

He then shifted into passing gear. While everybody expected him to be downcast, he appeared more confident than ever in the Commons. Meanwhile, though, the resignation of Bouchard, along with the looming deadline of June 23, was creating a feeling of panic at the highest level of governments across the country.

Premiers everywhere were almost begging Mulroney to hold a first ministers' conference. He had every intention of doing so. Although publicly he kept playing hard to get, sending Senator Lowell Murray to meet with the provincial leaders, and then claiming that he did not see room for compromise on the matter.

Finally, he pulled a move nobody expected. He decided to meet with every premier separately between May 24 and 28, just before the Gorbachev visit.

The first meeting was with David Peterson—and it may have been the most important, since all of them, in the end, were rather predictable.

That was when the Ontario premier pulled his Senate rabbit out of the hat for the first time. He told Mulroney that, if the negotiations got bogged down on Senate reform and there appeared to be no way out, he was ready to give away a certain number of Ontario's Senate seats.

Mulroney said that was very nice of him, but didn't think it would work.

Mikhail Gorbachev left the country on May 30. Mulroney then announced he would hold a first ministers' meeting, starting June 3.

When the premiers descended on Ottawa that Sunday night, it was to do what a lot of tourists do when they come to the capital: they went over to Hull.

Mulroney had decided to hold the first ministers' dinner at the Museum of Civilization, on the Quebec side of the Ottawa River.

It was a great TV shot. One after the other, the premiers and the prime minister paraded in front of a microphone set up on an outdoor terrace. In the background, you could see the cliff of Parliament Hill, and the Peace Tower. But, although nobody could see it, everyone knew that in between was a river, with Quebec on one side and Ontario on the other.

It was subliminal and deliberate. Mulroney, who had been turning up the heat on English Canada about the possibility of Quebec separating over the failure of the Meech Lake Accord, wanted to drive the point home. This was what it was all about.

Not much happened that night, as every participant in the closed meeting reiterated his position.

But, as much as some premiers had said that the meeting might last a few days, few really expected it to turn into the bargaining marathon it was—ending dramatically seven days later.

There have been a lot of stories about what "actually" happened behind those closed doors, during that crucial week in the history of Canada. Since the versions are inevitably tainted, depending on who you speak to and from which province, it's hard to know exactly what went on. Because there were only the eleven men there—with their advisers coming in when needed.

For a good part of the time, in fact, the first ministers weren't together at all, as aides did most of the bargaining and talking.

But there are the stories about how P.E.I. Premier Joe Ghiz called Clyde Wells "a prick." That may have been the greatest thing Ghiz ever said, but apparently he never said it. According to my information, he just told Wells, "Fuck you!" and the Newfoundland premier retorted, "Fuck you too!"

That's where another legend comes in; the one about Alberta Premier Don Getty "tackling" Wells to prevent him from leaving the meeting, after the exchange with Ghiz. I am told Getty simply stood up and asked everybody to calm down.

It was also at that point in the discussion, on the Thursday (day five), that Peterson took out his senate proposal, relinquishing six Senate seats from his province, to get a deal on possible senate reform.

Whatever happened, it came down to the Friday night, when eleven exhausted men thought they had reached a deal to save Meech and Canada.

As it turned out, they hadn't.

If you remember, that was the night every premier, except Clyde Wells, walked out of the meeting saying they had "an agreement in principle." The Newfoundland premier had discovered a "missing clause" in the final document.

In fact, he wasn't the one who discovered it. One of his lawyers did.

The clause had to do with Quebec's "distinct society." Wells had agreed not to define the distinct society clause, but wanted assurance that it would not supersede the Charter of Rights. The only concession Premier Robert Bourassa would make on that was to include, as an appendix to the deal, a letter from constitutional experts stating that the Charter was not affected in any way.

That was fine. But Wells also asked for another condition; that the distinct society clause be reviewed in ten years, pending court decisions on the matter.

But nobody seemed to know about this, except the federal officials and Wells's advisers.

You have to remember that this was a pressure cooker, the sixth day of a meeting among eleven men who were all on the edge of exhaustion, and knew they couldn't walk out without some kind of deal. A lot of things happen, and are said, in such an environment that people don't recall later.

The fact is, though, that Wells himself never saw the so-called "missing clause" when the final document was shown to him, somewhere around midnight on June 8. He was too tired to see anything. But his top lawyer spotted the omission.

And that was when the trouble started, while everybody still thought they had a deal. Wells felt he had been tricked, and went over to tell Mulroney about it.

The prime minister didn't have a clue what the Newfoundland premier was talking about, and couldn't believe it was all that important. Exhausted himself, he said, "Don't worry, Clyde, it will be taken care of."

Clyde was not amused. He walked out of the Ottawa Conference Centre at about two in the morning, and told the waiting media that he had a serious problem with the supposed deal.

What had happened? Had Mulroney deliberately tried to trick Clyde Wells, as he obviously thought?

I only have one version of that, but I believe it.

As they were drafting what should have been the final document, one federal official told another that Clyde Wells's concern about the ten years was not being addressed. Norman Spector simply said, "Fuck them."

Why? Probably because he thought it wasn't all that important and that, once the euphoria of a "save-the-country" deal hit, every premier, including Wells, would be too happy to complain.

Except that it sort of complicated things. It took another full day to get back to where the first ministers had been the night before. Finally, with Wells still holding out, Mulroney said that was it. He had Filmon's "thirteen days" in mind.

Wells signed the agreement, without signing.

Still, Mulroney thought he had it made. He had accomplished the impossible—one more time. He had rammed it through, all right. It wasn't perfect, he had lost Lucien Bouchard in the process, but with success comes success. It would all be arranged in the long run.

He already had plans to hold a special ceremony on Parliament Hill on June 23, which would, hopefully, coincide with the election of the new Liberal leader, Jean Chretien.

He giggled about it in private.

On the Sunday morning following the "deal," he got on the phone. He wanted to chat with anybody who would tell him how great it all was.

Among others, he talked to *Globe and Mail* editor-in-chief William Thorsell. That was one phone call too many. Somehow, Thorsell came away with a promise that Mulroney would give *The Globe* an interview the very next day, to mark the launching of its new-look edition.

The interview was done by columnist Jeffrey Simpson, bureau chief Graham Fraser, and top correspondent Susan Delacourt. Not exactly second-stringers.

The prime minister was in no shape to give an interview. He was both physically and mentally drained.

Furthermore, he was in an impossible position: he had to give straight answers, but he couldn't say too much, because three legislatures, including Newfoundland's, still had to vote on the deal. Any little slip could upset all of that.

As it turned out, it was a big slip.

Mulroney told the *Globe* reporters that he had set the date for the June 3-9 meeting on May 11. He said he had "counted backwards," and told his officials "that's when we roll all the dice."

It smacked not only of manipulation, but of a man boasting about it.

All hell broke loose in the Commons. Clyde Wells reacted predictably—although Mulroney phoned to calm him down, as soon as he saw *The Globe*'s story.

It was bad, bad, bad.

Mulroney then hit a deep depression. He locked himself into 24 Sussex, and conducted all the affairs of government from there, not showing up in the Commons until Nelson Mandela visited Ottawa, four sitting days later.

He had nobody to blame but himself, and he couldn't live with his own stupidity.

In his mind, he hadn't been gloating. He had simply explained how he had "counted backwards" to June 3. He felt he had to give the reporters "something" to chew on.

Now he himself had put Meech Lake in jeopardy.

In fact, all he had really lost then was what we call "the edge," in gambling and politics. From then on, whatever happened, the premiers would look at him warily, wondering if he was going to boast about having screwed them later.

And that edge might have been what Mulroney needed two weeks later, when the clock ran out on Meech Lake.

But, as the country knows, the Meech Lake Accord was really killed by one man, an aboriginal by the name of Elijah Harper, NDP member of the Manitoba Legislature.

Nobody could do anything about Harper, because everybody knew he had a just cause. And nobody had any plan, at the federal level, to change that.

Mulroney did throw a tantrum at one point, claiming that Premier Filmon could force a vote if he really wanted to, but it didn't make any moral sense.

Still, while his officials were looking at possible options beyond the June 23 deadline, Mulroney went to the Newfoundland House of Assembly to defend the deal, two days before that. He gave a masterful speech.

That night, he had dinner with Clyde Wells. I hear it was a rather boring, but courteous, affair. He was feeling good.

Then came the news that the Manitoba Legislature would adjourn at noon on the Friday, which meant that Elijah Harper's one-man filibuster had worked. Meech Lake would die.

That Friday morning, Senator Lowell Murray found out from Clyde Wells that the Newfoundland premier planned to cancel the vote and let his people off the hook that way.

Mulroney went berserk. He scrambled for solutions. He wanted his advisers to give him something, anything!

Instead of going before the cameras himself and demanding that Newfoundland hold the vote, despite what was happening in Manitoba, he sent Lowell Murray.

The senator then unveiled, before the mesmerized national media, a plan that could have only bee concocted by desperate people who had lost control of the situation.

He said that the federal government would consult the Supreme Court, to determine whether the June 23 deadline was absolute or if it applied only to Quebec, the first province to have approved the Meech Lake Accord, back in 1987. If it sounds complicated, that's because it is.

I'll spare you the details, except to say this: the whole idea was to make sure that Newfoundland would vote on the issue, because the Manitoba problem was only a matter of time. If the deadline was extended, then the approval by the Legislature was a mere formality.

Such was not the case in Newfoundland, where Wells still opposed the deal and held a majority of seats—although he was committed to letting the members of his caucus vote with their consciences.

The Murray intervention did nothing to change things. Elijah Harper made the Manitoba Legislature adjourn, and Clyde killed the vote.

At that point, Mulroney still wouldn't say die. There had to be another way.

Finally it was Paul Tellier, the Clerk of the Privy Council, who brought him back to his senses and told him he had to accept that it was over.

Mulroney was a crushed man. All he had wanted to do, he said, was to give everybody his or her place in Canada. All he had wanted to accomplish was to keep the talent of Quebec in a greater, bigger country. He just wanted everyone to feel like they belonged. That's all he ever intended to do.

The next day, Saturday, June 23, he went on national TV to admit what Tellier had told him: he had failed.

Two days later in Montreal, 500,000 people took to the streets with fleur-de-lis flags, to proclaim Quebec's unwritten independence on the national holiday of St-Jean Baptiste. More people than there are on the whole island of Newfoundland.

Brian saw it on TV and thought, *I told them so.*

But the real nagging thought was that, had Clyde Wells held the vote in his House of Assembly, Mulroney knew he would have won it by two votes.

Hell of a way to lose a country.

## Epilogue

Were we all fooled by this clever, charming, machiavellian man? Not once, but twice?

Did he ruin the country, because of his personal ambition and agenda? Or did he make the best he could of a messy situation?

Could things have been different?

This story ends with the failure of the Meech Lake Accord. But politics has very few beginnings and ends. The wheel never stops turning. It is not like a hockey game, or even a hockey season.

That's why politicians thrive in the rare situations where they can set a goal and try to reach it, such as an election or a leadership convention. But those remain illusions, in the greater scheme of things. Because, on the morning after an election, life goes on—and life is the playing field of politics, with its changing rules, moods and unexpected events.

Brian Mulroney's greatest strength is that he understands this. Because he knows the wheel keeps turning, he never says die. There will always be another chance.

His greatest weakness is that he tries to cheat at it.

He has succumbed to the temptation of every politician who has tried to master The Beast: Television. He has confused short-lived public-relations triumphs with widespread public approval.

In the course of winning two elections, he has mesmerized the people with brilliant battlefield tactics—winnning almost every skirmish until the Meech Lake defeat. And there, like Napoleon at Waterloo, he still wanted to fight on when it was clearly over. Maybe because losing never even entered his mind.

After six years of Brian Mulroney, Canadians have sized him up as a scheming, conniving politician, who comes out with the truth only when he gets caught.

That may not be the man I have known, but Mulroney dug his own grave.

Since he wouldn't let people look beyond the shining armour he wanted them to see, but which was bound to rust when things got bad, they drew their own conclusions about what kind of man their prime minister was.

When he tried to play catch-up and make them believe he was a lot better than that, many of them simply didn't listen. Their minds were made up.

That, in the end, is why he lost the Meech Lake battle. Clyde Wells could never have blocked the accord if he hadn't known that the prime minister's unpopularity with the voters was working in favour of Newfoundland. He never could have played his righteousness against Mulroney's secretive and calculating style.

It was a heavy price to pay, for Mulroney and the country. But it was a disaster that was just waiting to happen.

Since his leadership was based on image, when the mirage dissipated there was very little left.

He had won the people's votes. But he had forgotten about the most important thing: their hearts.

Maybe he just didn't know how to do it. Maybe it was really too hard for him to go out there and just be himself before the cameras that he depended on so much. Maybe he just never had it.

On February 17, 1990, Christine and I got married—both for the second time. Like most of my life, the wedding was sort of, well, wild—with me leading the charge.

Two days later, on February 19, as we were getting ready to leave on a honeymoon, when I intended to start serious work on this book, I got a phone call.

When I heard the familiar, nasal, female voice at the end of the line, I thought I was hallucinating. "Monsieur Gratton, the prime minister would like to speak to you."

As I had done so many times, I said "Yes," and waited.

It was him, phoning to congratulate me and my wife on our wedding.

He said, before delivering the message, "You are speaking to a guy who needs all the taxpayers he can get!"

I was touched. Not so much that he thought of it, but that he had the guts to phone. One year before that, he wasn't even talking to me.

I hung up the phone, thinking about what an exceptional man he was—if only he would let himself be.

But maybe I was fooled, too.

It doesn't really matter.

Whether I was or not is quite unimportant to me.

When I think about it all, I just wish it could have been different.